EASY
COMFORT
FOOD

EASY COMFORT FOOD

Illustrated
Recipes &
Stories of
Home

BILL HO
@BILL8CAFE

Marshall Cavendish
Cuisine

Editor: Lo Yi Min
Designer: Bernard Go Kwang Meng

Copyright © 2020 Marshall Cavendish International (Asia) Private Limited
Text and illustrations © Bill Ho

Published by Marshall Cavendish Cuisine
An imprint of Marshall Cavendish International

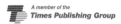

A member of the
Times Publishing Group

Other Marshall Cavendish Offices:
Marshall Cavendish Corporation, 99 White Plains Road, Tarrytown NY 10591-9001, USA •
Marshall Cavendish International (Thailand) Co Ltd, 253 Asoke, 12th Flr, Sukhumvit 21 Road,
Klongtoey Nua, Wattana, Bangkok 10110, Thailand • Marshall Cavendish (Malaysia) Sdn Bhd,
Times Subang, Lot 46, Subang Hi-Tech Industrial Park, Batu Tiga, 40000 Shah Alam,
Selangor Darul Ehsan, Malaysia.

Marshall Cavendish is a registered trademark of Times Publishing Limited

National Library Board, Singapore Cataloguing in Publication Data

Names: Ho, Bill.
Title: Easy comfort food : illustrated recipes & stories of home / Bill Ho @Bill8Cafe.
Description: Singapore : Marshall Cavendish Cuisine, [2020]
Identifiers: OCN 1128107399 | ISBN 978-981-48-6848-8 (paperback)
Subjects: LCSH: Quick and easy cooking. | LCGFT: Cookbooks.
Classification: DDC 641.555–dc23

Printed in Singapore

To Mum, Dad and the others who
have guided me through life.
These recipes are inspired by them and
each time I cook or eat these dishes, I think about
them and the memories we've shared.

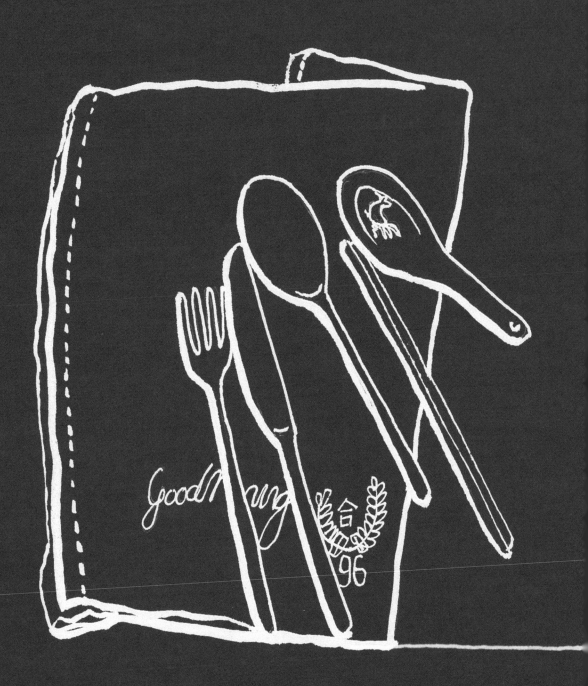

09
Introduction

11
Acknowledgements

13
Light Bites
and
Party Snacks

49
Salads
and
Soups

75
Easy Dishes for
a Small Family

110
About the
Author

112
Weights and
Measures

CONTENTS

INTRODUCTION

This cookbook is a reflection of two of my passions: art and food.

As a kid I loved to draw and I aspired to be an artist. When I grew older and had to pick what to study at university, it was easy — I enrolled in a graphic design course. However, when I graduated, it was difficult to get a job related to graphic design or art.

In order to get by, I started work as a waiter in a Chinese restaurant. One day, when the kitchen was short of staff, I stepped in to help and discovered I enjoyed cooking very much. Long story short, I put on the apron and didn't look back. After working in many kitchens of different cuisines, I opened my own café.

All through the years of learning to be a chef and running a food business, I continued to paint and sketch. And I still do today, because drawing and cooking are two wonderful creative outlets.

I hope that through this cookbook, more people will share my love for them, especially cooking, which is often seen as something tedious and time-consuming these days. The recipes I share here have been tweaked to suit the modern busy home cook. You will find options for weeknight dinners, from one-dish meals to hearty soups and light yet filling salads.

Many of the recipes were inspired by what I had when I was growing up in a kampung in Malaysia. For me, making these dishes always brings back wonderful memories associated with them. I hope you'll try them and make your own memories sharing them with family and friends.

Bill Ho

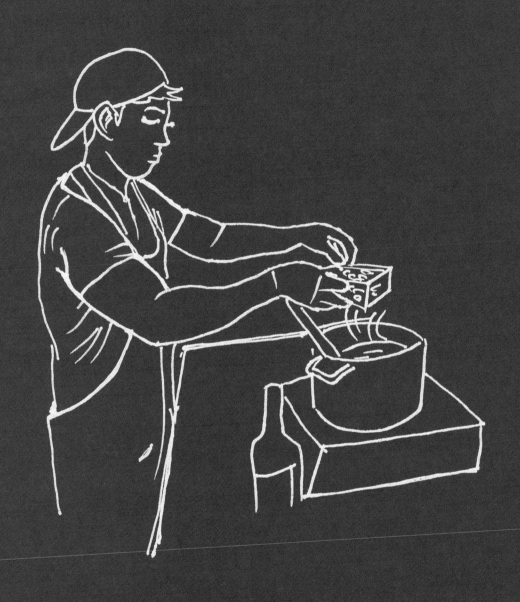

ACKNOWLEDGEMENTS

Thank you Mum and Dad, and all those who have spent time and effort guiding me all these years.

A special thanks goes to Irene Tan who helped me on this project.

I would also like to thank my editor, who found me through Instagram and approached me to do a cookbook. I'm glad that we persevered and made this a reality!

Soft Dinner Rolls   14

Home-style Char Siew   17

Baked Char Siew Buns   18

Popcorn Chicken   21

Yong Tau Foo   22

Wonton Skin Kuih Pie Tee   25

Chicken Marinara Wonton Tapas   26

Chilli Oil Dumplings   29

Siew Mai   30

Easy Chicken Satay   33

Savoury Vegetarian Pancakes   34

Vegan Patties   37

Har Cheong Gai   38

Homemade Fish Balls   41

Potato Gratin   42

Kee Chang   45

Kaya   46

LIGHT BITES AND PARTY SNACKS

Soft Dinner Rolls

Makes 36 buns

1 kg bread flour

500 g cake flour

10 g caster sugar

1 tsp salt

50 g yeast

2 eggs

50 g unsalted butter, melted

100 ml milk

650 ml water

In a large bowl, place both flours, sugar, salt and yeast. Stir to mix well.

Reserve 1 egg for making an egg wash. Beat the remaining egg and add to flour mixture. Add butter and milk, then mix well. Gradually add water, stirring to form a sticky dough.

Turn dough onto a lightly floured work surface. Dust hands lightly with flour and knead dough until it is smooth and soft. This should take about 15 minutes.

Transfer to a large bowl and cover with a damp towel, followed by cling film. Leave to rise at room temperature for 1 hour, until dough has doubled in size.

Divide equally into 36 portions and roll each portion into a ball. Arrange slightly apart on greased baking trays, cover with a damp towel and leave to rise again for 1 hour.

Preheat oven to 200°C.

Bake for 15 minutes until golden brown. For a richer colour, lightly beat the remaining egg and brush on top of buns, then bake for another minute.

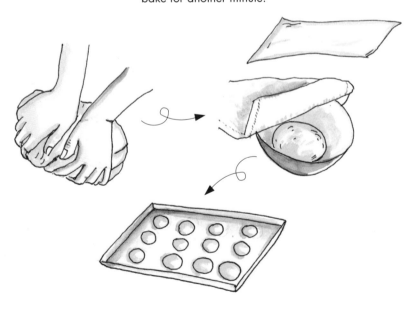

The first time I made bread on my own was making these dinner rolls. A pastry chef I worked with in a tea lounge was kind enough to share this recipe with me. As someone who grew up in a kampung and only knew bread to mean the traditional sliced white loaf eaten with margarine and *kaya* (coconut jam), I was quite overwhelmed with emotion when I tasted bread I had made for the first time! This is a big batch, but it can be kept frozen, and reheated in the oven when needed.

Also known as Cantonese roast barbecue pork, this is one of my favourite pork dishes. I love the smoky char on its edges! *Char siew* can be served with rice or wonton noodles, but you can also have it as a cold dish served with garlic chilli sauce. While working on the dishes for my café, I discovered that *char siew* goes well with red wine — it's East meets West at its best.

Home-style Char Siew

Makes about 800 g

800 g pork loin

3 cloves garlic, peeled
  and minced

2 tsp five-spice powder

1 tsp ground white pepper

1 tsp salt

2 Tbsp sugar

125 ml water

3 Tbsp oyster sauce

2 Tbsp tomato sauce

1 Tbsp sweet chilli sauce

2 Tbsp dark soy sauce

2 Tbsp Shaoxing wine

Place pork loin in a bowl. Add garlic, five-spice powder, pepper and salt to the bowl. Rub all over pork and set aside to marinate.

In a saucepan over low heat, combine sugar and water. Cook until sugar is melted and caramelised. Stir in all the sauces and Shaoxing wine. Cook for about 5 minutes until mixture is sticky and fragrant.

Pour sauce over pork, cover and leave to marinate overnight in the refrigerator.

Preheat oven to 200°C. Prepare a roasting pan or rack.

Place pork in prepared pan and reserve marinade for glazing. Roast for 10 minutes, then brush pork with more marinade. Rotate pork a quarter turn in the pan and roast for another 10 minutes. Repeat glazing, rotating and roasting once more. The surface of the pork should be slightly charred at this point. Brush with more glaze and roast for a final 5 minutes.

Baked Char Siew Buns

Makes 12 buns

FILLING

2 Tbsp cornflour

150 ml chicken stock or water

1 Tbsp olive oil

1 small onion, peeled and diced

300 g *char siew*, diced
  (see page 17)

1 Tbsp oyster sauce

1 Tbsp light soy sauce

1 tsp dark soy sauce

1 tsp Shaoxing wine

1 tsp sesame oil

2 tsp sugar

1 tsp salt

2 stalks spring onion,
  finely chopped

DOUGH

1 kg bread flour

500 g cake flour

10 g caster sugar

A pinch of salt

50 g yeast

2 eggs

50 g unsalted butter, melted

100 ml milk

650 ml water

Prepare filling. Mix cornflour with chicken stock or water in a small bowl. Set aside.

In a frying pan, heat olive oil over medium heat and fry onion and *char siew* until onion is fragrant. Stir in the sauces, Shaoxing wine, sesame oil, sugar and salt, then cook until fragrant. Mix in spring onions.

Add cornflour mixture, stir to combine and simmer until thickened. Divide equally into 12 portions and set aside in the refrigerator.

Prepare dough. In a large bowl, place both flours, sugar, salt and yeast. Stir to mix well.

Reserve 1 egg for making an egg wash. Beat the remaining egg and add to flour mixture. Add butter and milk, then mix well. Gradually add water, stirring to form a sticky dough.

Turn dough onto a lightly floured work surface. Dust hands lightly with flour and knead dough until it is smooth and soft. This should take about 15 minutes.

Transfer to a large bowl and cover with a damp towel, followed by cling film. Leave to rise at room temperature for 1 hour, until dough is double in size.

Divide equally into 12 portions and roll each portion into a ball. Arrange slightly apart on greased baking trays, cover with a damp towel and leave to rise again for 1 hour.

Flatten a dough ball into a disc. Place 2 Tbsp filling (or more if you prefer) in its centre, then wrap dough around filling. Pinch edges to seal dough and roll gently to smooth out surface. Repeat to make 12 buns.

Arrange buns about 5 cm apart on greased baking trays, then spray lightly with water. Cover and leave to rise for 30 minutes.

Preheat oven to 180°C.

Bake for 15 minutes until golden brown. For a richer colour, lightly beat the remaining egg and brush on top of buns, then bake for another minute.

You can make good use of your home-style *char siew* with this! When people talk about *char siew* buns, they usually mean the steamed ones that are always served at dim sum places. This baked version is less common but just as tasty. The slightly crispy and chewy crust of the bun adds a nice contrast to the filling.

This is the perfect snack to serve at parties because it's boneless (no holding onto bones awkwardly), not messy (unlike sauce-coated chicken), and super addictive. Plus, it goes well with beer or wine. I promise, this will be a crowd favourite among all ages!

Popcorn Chicken

Makes about 500 g

500 g chicken breast,
   cut into bite-sized pieces

2 tsp salt

1 tsp ground white pepper

200 ml milk

500 g all-purpose (plain) flour

2 tsp chicken powder

$^{1}/_{2}$ tsp curry powder

1 tsp ground paprika + more
   for garnishing

1 egg

Vegetable oil for deep-frying

1 tsp chilli powder

Place chicken in a bowl. Rub with salt and pepper, then add milk and leave to soak for 30 minutes.

In a separate large bowl, combine flour, chicken powder, curry powder and 1 tsp paprika. Stir to mix well. Lightly beat egg in another bowl.

If baking chicken, preheat the oven to 200°C.

Drain chicken. Dip a chicken piece into the egg to coat evenly, then dredge it through the flour mixture. Coat with another layer of egg and flour mixture, then set aside. Repeat to coat all the chicken pieces.

Arrange on a greased baking tray and bake for 12 minutes until golden brown.

If deep-frying chicken, heat enough oil in a saucepan over medium-high heat. When oil is hot enough, add chicken and deep-fry until golden brown. Do this in batches so that you do not overcrowd the pot. Remove chicken with a slotted spoon and set aside on paper towels to drain excess oil.

Sprinkle with chilli powder and more paprika. Serve warm.

Yong Tau Foo

Makes 8 portions as a snack
or 4 portions for a meal

1 brinjal (aubergine)

10 ladies' fingers

10 red or green chillies

4–5 cakes *tau kwa* (firm tofu)

10 *tau pok*
(deep-fried beancurd puff)

Vegetable oil for deep-frying

Spring onion for garnishing,
chopped

FILLING

300 g prawns, peeled and
tails removed, finely chopped

700–900 g minced pork

20 g garlic, peeled and minced

20 g *mui heong* (dried salted fish),
finely chopped

1 stalk spring onion, finely chopped

1 tsp ground white pepper

1 Tbsp salt

1 Tbsp light soy sauce

SAUCE

10 g garlic, peeled and minced

Vegetable oil as needed

2 Tbsp *tau cheo* (fermented soy
bean paste)

2 Tbsp oyster sauce

1 Tbsp Shaoxing wine

250 ml water

1 Tbsp light soy sauce

1 tsp sugar

1 tsp salt

2 Tbsp potato starch

Prepare filling. Place all ingredients for filling in a bowl and mix well. Using your hands, gather mixture into a ball. Scoop up mixture and slap it against a chopping board. Do this 4–5 times until the mixture's texture is firm. Set aside.

Cut brinjal into 2.5-cm slices. Make a horizontal slit halfway down each slice so it looks like a half-opened sandwich.

Make a slit down the length of each lady's finger and chilli. Remove seeds carefully.

Cut *tau kwa* block into triangle halves, then carefully use a spoon to scoop out the centre of each half. Cut *tau pok* into triangle halves.

Spoon filling into vegetables, chillies, *tau kwa* and *tau pok*. Pat filling down firmly, but do not overstuff each piece.

Heat enough oil for deep-frying in a large saucepan. When oil is hot enough, deep-fry *yong tau foo* until golden brown. Transfer onto a steaming rack in a wok and add enough water without covering *yong tau foo*. Cover and steam over high heat for 12 minutes. Set aside in serving bowl.

Prepare sauce. Place garlic in a saucepan and add enough oil to cover garlic. Fry over low heat until aromatic. Add *tau cheo*, oyster sauce, Shaoxing wine and water. Season with soy sauce, sugar and salt. Bring to a boil and simmer for 2 minutes.

Remove from heat and stir in potato starch to thicken sauce. Pour over *yong tau foo* and garnish with chopped spring onion.

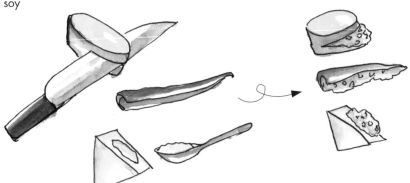

Yong tau foo is a Hakka dish made by stuffing vegetables and tofu with a seafood and meat paste. My mum used to prepare this so that my siblings and I would eat our vegetables. We loved eating meat but not vegetables, so with this dish, we had no choice but to have both at the same time.

I've always liked the traditional *kuih pie tee*, the Nyonya snack made of crispy pastry cups filled with sweet and savoury stir-fried vegetables. The individual portions make it so easy to eat and perfect for tapas. I found that making the pastry cups from scratch was a bit too much of a hassle, so I thought of shaping them with wonton skins instead. Although you can buy ready-made pastry cups off the shelves, it's quite fun to get crafty and shape your own.

Wonton Skin Kuih Pie Tee

Makes about 20 cups

Vegetable oil for frying

50 g dried prawns

500 g *mangkuang* (jicama),
   peeled and shredded

1 carrot, peeled and shredded)

100 g bean sprouts, tailed

A pinch of sugar

1 tsp fish sauce

2 tsp + a pinch salt

1 egg, beaten and seasoned with
   a pinch of salt

1 Tbsp Shaoxing wine

20–30 prawns, shells on

Butter or olive oil for greasing

1 packet store-bought
   wonton skins

1 head lettuce, leaves separated,
   washed and dried

Coriander leaves for garnishing,
   chopped

1 red chilli, de-seeded, sliced

CHILLI SAUCE

8 red chillies

20 g garlic, peeled

1 thumb-sized knob ginger, peeled

1 tsp sugar

5 Tbsp lime juice + more to taste

2 tsp fish sauce

In a large pan, heat some oil over medium heat and fry dried prawns until fragrant, then add *mangkuang*, carrot and bean sprouts. Fry until vegetables are tender, for about 8–10 minutes. Season with a pinch of sugar, fish sauce and 2 tsp salt, then remove filling from heat and set aside.

Add enough oil to a frying pan to coat it thinly. Heat oil until hot, remove from heat and wipe off excess oil with a paper towel. Pour egg into pan and spread thinly. Let the residual heat cook the egg, about 30 seconds. Gently flip omelette, cooking a few seconds on this side to set, then remove from pan. Leave aside to cool before rolling up omelette and cutting into strips.

Fill a large pot with water, adding a pinch of salt and Shaoxing wine. Bring to a boil before adding prawns. Cook until prawns start to rise to the surface and the water comes to a boil again. Transfer prawns into a bowl of iced water. When prawns are cooled, peel and slice into halves. Set aside.

Prepare chilli sauce. Blend chillies, garlic, ginger, sugar, lime juice and fish sauce together. Add more lime juice if you prefer it more tart.

Preheat the oven to 180°C. Grease a mini muffin pan with butter or olive oil. Place a wonton skin over a muffin cup and, using your finger, press its centre into the cup base. Arrange skin to form pleats on the sides of the cup. Repeat to use up wonton skins, then bake empty wonton skin cups for 12 minutes until crispy. Leave to cool in pan on a wire rack.

Tear or cut lettuce leaves into small pieces and place a few pieces at the bottom of each cup. Fill cup to about four-fifths full with filling, and top with omelette strips and a prawn half.

Garnish with coriander leaves and sliced chilli. Serve with chilli sauce.

Chicken Marinara Wonton Tapas

Makes about 20 cups

Butter or olive oil for greasing

1 packet store-bought
   wonton skins

2 Tbsp olive oil

600 g skinless chicken thigh,
   diced

1 onion, peeled and diced

10 g garlic, peeled and minced

2 tomatoes, diced

4 Tbsp tomato paste

5 g basil leaves, roughly chopped
   or torn

2 tsp salt

1 tsp ground black pepper

150 g mozzarella cheese,
   shredded

Preheat the oven to 180°C. Grease a mini muffin pan with butter or olive oil. Place a wonton skin over a muffin cup and, using your finger, press its centre into the cup base. Arrange skin to form pleats on the sides of the cup. Repeat to use up wonton skins, then bake empty wonton skin cups for 12 minutes until crispy. Leave to cool in pan on a wire rack.

Heat oil in a saucepan over medium heat, then fry chicken, onion and garlic until fragrant. Stir in tomatoes and tomato paste, ensuring chicken pieces are coated thoroughly, then cook for 5 minutes.

Preheat the oven to 200°C. Fill each wonton cup with chicken mixture until nearly full. Top each cup with 2 pieces of basil leaves, and cover with mozzarella cheese.

Bake for 7–8 minutes, until cheese is melted and golden brown.

Garnish with remaining basil leaves and serve warm.

Once I discovered how to make crispy pastry cups at home using store-bought wonton skin, it opened up various possibilities of fillings that could be served this way as a tapas dish. I imagined having mini pizzas at parties, but in this form so that they would be easier to hold and eat, and that's how this dish came to be. You can also make this using leftovers in your fridge – season and garnish with whatever you like!

I confess that I don't really like vinegar, though many people do. It's not that I don't enjoy sour flavours — I like lemon and lime juices added to dishes. It's the sharpness in the smell of vinegar I find difficult to enjoy. But when I had my first plate of chilli oil dumplings, I was pleasantly surprised by how the combination of vinegar with garlic, chilli oil and soy sauce made a dressing that went so well with dumplings.

Chilli Oil Dumplings

Makes 25–30 dumplings

500–700 g pork, minced

200 g peeled prawns, tails removed, minced

10 g garlic, peeled and minced

1 stalk spring onion, finely chopped + more for garnishing

1 Tbsp oyster sauce

2 Tbsp light soy sauce

1 Tbsp rice wine

1 Tbsp all-purpose (plain) flour

1 packet store-bought wonton skins

CHILLI OIL

10 g garlic, peeled and minced

20 g red chilli, finely diced

10 g dried chilli flakes

2 Tbsp black vinegar

1 Tbsp light soy sauce

1 tsp sugar

$^1/_2$ cup olive oil

6–7 dried chillies, chopped

10 g Szechuan peppercorns

Prepare chilli oil. Mix all ingredients except olive oil, dried chillies and peppercorns in a bowl.

Heat oil in a saucepan over medium heat, and fry dried chillies and peppercorns until the mixture is red and fragrant.

Pour hot chilli oil over garlic chilli mixture and mix well to combine. Set aside until needed.

Prepare dumplings. In a large bowl, mix pork, prawn, garlic, spring onions, both sauces and rice wine together. Cover and refrigerate for at least 30 minutes.

To assemble dumplings, mix flour into a bowl of water to make a solution.

Place a teaspoonful of filling in the centre of a wonton skin. Moisten the corners of the skin with a finger dipped in flour solution. Gather the corners into the centre, and bunch them together to seal the dumpling. Repeat to use up wonton skins and filling.

Bring a pot of water to a boil and poach dumplings in boiling water. The dumplings are cooked when they start to float. Drain and transfer to a serving bowl. Pour chilli oil over, garnish with spring onion and serve.

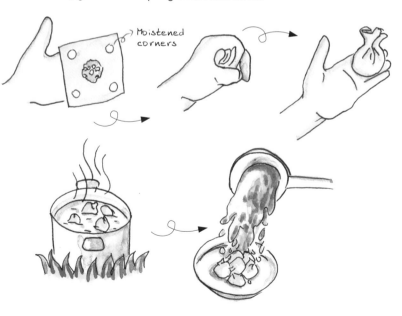

Moistened corners

Siew Mai

Makes about 20 dumplings

1 packet store-bought
   wonton skins

A handful of dried goji berries
   (wolfberries), rinsed

Garlic chilli sauce for serving

FILLING

700–900 g pork, minced

300 g prawns, peeled and tails
   removed, minced

50 g carrot, finely diced

80 g shiitake mushrooms,
   finely diced

4 tsp salt

1 tsp sugar

1 Tbsp oyster sauce

2 Tbsp light soy sauce

2 Tbsp rice wine

Prepare filling. Place all ingredients for filling in a bowl and mix well. Cover and refrigerate for at least 30 minutes.

Prepare a steamer. Line a steamer tray with a clean muslin cloth, or with Chinese cabbage leaves if you prefer.

To assemble, place a tablespoonful of filling in the centre of a wonton skin. Moisten the edge of the skin with a wet finger, then begin pleating skin by pushing one part of the edge towards the centre and pressing the gathered pleats together. Leave the top uncovered and decorate with 3 goji berries. Repeat to use up filling.

Arrange *siew mai* on steamer tray and steam over high heat for 10–12 minutes.

Serve hot with garlic chilli sauce.

Like so many people, I must order
siew mai when I dine at a dim sum
restaurant. However, I find the individual
siew mai a little too small for my liking
sometimes. The best thing about making
my own *siew mai* at home is making
them a little bigger, packed with more
goodies! I opted to garnish with goji
berries because they are healthier and
readily available.

I remember my first taste of chicken satay. It was at a night market in Cheras, Kuala Lumpur, and the lady grilling the skewers over the hot charcoal was fanning the fire with a bamboo fan. That aroma of the caramelised, slightly charred meat wafted over and got my attention right away. Dipped in a generous amount of spicy peanut sauce, that satay really made an impression on me. My version can be made at home without a charcoal grill, but it's also great for having at barbecues.

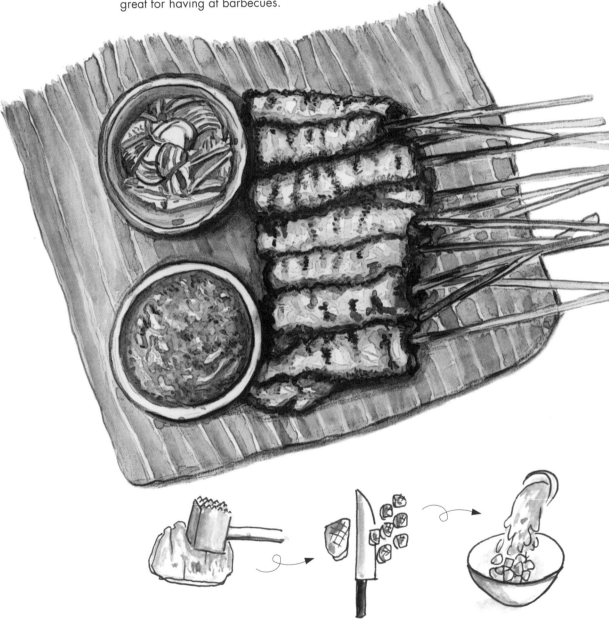

Easy Chicken Satay

Makes about 20 sticks

1–1.5 kg boneless chicken thigh

1 egg, lightly beaten

3 stalks lemongrass

2 lime leaves

20 g ground turmeric

10 g curry powder

5 g coriander powder

5 g ground paprika

4 tsp salt

2 tsp sugar

PEANUT SAUCE

20 g garlic, peeled

50 g shallots, peeled

50 g galangal, peeled

2 stalks lemongrass

200 g red chillies

100 g dried chillies

10 g coriander powder

4–5 Tbsp vegetable oil

350 g chunky, lightly sweetened
   peanut butter

250 ml tamarind juice, obtained
   from mixing 4 Tbsp tamarind
   paste with 250 ml water

60 ml water

Sugar to taste

Salt to taste

Sweet dark soy sauce
   to taste

Prepare chicken a day ahead. Using a mallet, tenderise chicken thigh on both sides. Cut chicken thigh into cubes, place in a bowl and mix in egg. Leave to marinate for 30 minutes.

Place lemongrass, lime leaves, turmeric, curry and coriander powders, paprika, salt and sugar in a blender. Blend to form a paste. Rub paste onto chicken cubes, cover and chill overnight to marinate.

Prepare peanut sauce. Place garlic, shallots, galangal, lemongrass, red chillies, dried chillies and coriander powder in a blender. Blend to form a paste.

Heat oil in a saucepan over low to medium heat. Add paste and fry until fragrant before adding peanut butter, tamarind juice and water. Stir to combine and season with sugar, salt and sweet dark soy sauce to taste. Simmer for 10 minutes over low heat. Set aside.

To cook satay, thread chicken cubes onto bamboo skewers.

Heat a clean frying pan over low heat until pan is very hot. Lay skewered chicken in the pan and cook for 5–7 minutes, flipping skewers midway. Cook until chicken is lightly charred on both sides. Alternatively, grill satay over charcoal grill until chicken is lightly charred on both sides, about 5–7 minutes.

Serve with peanut sauce.

Savoury Vegetarian Pancakes

Makes 6 pancakes

500 g all-purpose (plain) flour

A pinch of sugar

Salt as needed

Water as needed

3 Tbsp olive oil

50 g carrot, peeled and diced

50 g shiitake mushrooms, diced

150 g chives, finely chopped

Place flour, sugar and a pinch of salt in a large mixing bowl and stir with a chopstick to combine. Gradually drizzle in 125 ml hot water, stirring continuously in one direction. The flour should clump together.

Gradually add 250 ml cold water, stirring continuously in one direction until a sticky dough forms and the flour is fully incorporated. You should be able to mould it into a ball.

Lightly dust both hands with flour before kneading dough until it is smooth. Form dough into a ball, then cover bowl with a cloth followed by cling film. Leave to rest for 30 minutes.

In the meantime, heat 2 Tbsp oil in a frying pan and stir-fry carrot. Add mushrooms, followed by chives, then cook until chives are wilted. Season with salt to taste. Set side.

Divide dough into 6 equal portions. On a lightly dusted work surface, roll out a portion thinly into a rectangular strip. Spread $1/2$ Tbsp vegetable filling on the strip and roll it up from one end to form a roll.

Flatten each roll to form a disc.

Heat 1 Tbsp oil in a frying pan over medium heat. Pan-fry each disc until golden brown on both sides.

When I was in India for a meditation retreat, I spent five days in a temple without my mobile phone and any communication to the world outside. I was served two vegetarian meals a day: the first at 6 a.m. and the second at 11 a.m. The first two days there were pretty rough, but then I got used to it. Of course, as I went for many hours without food from one day to the next, whatever I ate tasted pretty delicious! I particularly enjoyed a savoury pancake, so I made my own when I returned home.

Many people who choose to adopt a vegan diet are animal lovers or environmentalists. Having a lot of respect for how they choose to live by their principles, I developed a vegan patty recipe. This is sometimes served at my café.

Vegan Patties

Makes 12 patties

1 Tbsp olive oil

50 g yellow onion, peeled and finely chopped

80 g cauliflower, finely chopped

50 g carrot, peeled and finely chopped

100 g shiitake mushrooms, roughly chopped

80 g instant oatmeal

1 cake *tau kwa* (firm tofu), minced

20 g garlic, peeled and minced

2 Tbsp vegetarian oyster sauce

2 tsp ground turmeric

2 tsp coriander powder

1 tsp curry powder

80 g all-purpose (plain) flour

Heat oil in a frying pan over medium-low heat and fry onion until crispy and golden brown. Transfer to a large bowl.

Add cauliflower, carrot, mushrooms, oatmeal, *tau kwa* and garlic to fried onion. Mix with a spatula to combine evenly.

Mix in oyster sauce, turmeric, coriander and curry powders.

Drain liquid from mixture. Add flour to absorb any excess moisture and bind the loose mixture together.

Divide mixture into 12 equal portions, using your hand to mould each one into a disc.

To pan-fry patties, place them in a frying pan and add enough oil to cover patties. Pan-fry over low to medium heat for 3–5 minutes until golden brown.

To bake patties, preheat the oven to 150°C. Arrange patties on a greased baking pan and bake for 5–7 minutes until golden brown.

Serve as a filling in sandwiches or burgers, or cut patty into bite-sized pieces, accompanied with sweet chilli sauce on the side.

Har Cheong Gai

Makes 6–8 pieces

2 Tbsp dried prawn paste
(*belacan*)

10 g dried prawns, finely blended

10 g garlic, peeled and minced

2 tsp curry powder + more
for garnishing

1 tsp ground white pepper

1 tsp fish sauce

6–8 chicken wings

Vegetable oil for deep-frying

150 g all-purpose (plain) flour

10 g dried chilli flakes

Sweet chilli sauce for serving

In a large bowl, mix prawn paste, dried prawns, garlic, curry powder, pepper and fish sauce to form a marinade.

Place chicken wings in marinade, cover and leave for at least 30 minutes or overnight.

To deep-fry chicken wings, heat enough oil for deep-frying in a saucepan. If baking chicken wings, preheat the oven to 180°C.

While oil is heating or oven is preheating, place flour on a large plate. Remove chicken wings from marinade and dredge through flour.

When oil is hot enough, deep-fry chicken wings until golden brown.

To bake, arrange chicken wings on a baking tray and bake for 15 minutes until golden brown.

Sprinkle with chilli flakes and curry powder. Serve hot with sweet chilli sauce, if desired.

Also known as prawn paste chicken, this is a popular fried chicken snack in Malaysia and Singapore. If you aren't used to cooking with dried prawn paste (*belacan*), you might find it quite pungent, but it's utterly delicious once it's cooked. Dried prawn paste is what gives this fried chicken its special salty, lightly fermented and savoury taste.

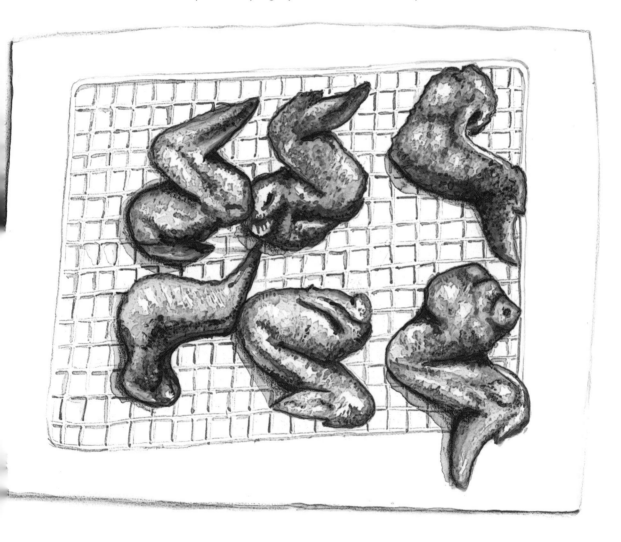

Fish balls are the go-to ingredients to add to a meal for busy families. They are also really easy to pick up at wet markets (fresher) and supermarkets (more convenient). However, these commercial fish balls tend to be made with a lot of other fillers. To appreciate the taste of fish in your fish balls, you can make them at home fairly easily. It can be a little tedious to make the fish paste, but you can save time by purchasing fillets or having the fishmonger debone the fish for you.

Homemade Fish Balls

Makes 20 fish balls

Vegetable oil as needed

2 yellow onions, peeled and finely diced

1 tsp + 1 Tbsp salt

800 g–1 kg yellowtail or mackerel fillets

1 egg white

50 g garlic, peeled and finely chopped

20 g ginger, peeled and finely chopped

2 Tbsp oyster sauce

2 Tbsp rice wine

4 Tbsp white pepper

50 g all-purpose (plain) flour

Heat oil in a frying pan over medium-low heat and fry onions with 1 tsp salt until onions are crispy and golden brown. Drain on paper towels and set aside.

Mince fish meat using a knife, then transfer to a large bowl.

Add egg white, fried onions, garlic and ginger, then mix well. Season mixture with oyster sauce, rice wine and pepper. Using your hand, stir the mixture in one direction for about 5–6 minutes. Add flour and stir for another 5 minutes.

Using your hands, gather mixture into a ball. Scoop up mixture and slap it against a chopping board. Do this 5–6 times until the mixture's texture is springy. Cover and refrigerate for 30 minutes.

To shape fish balls, scoop a tablespoonful of the mixture and roll it into a ball. Repeat to use up mixture.

To deep-fry, coat fish balls lightly with plain flour before adding to hot oil. To cook in soup, bring soup to a boil before adding fish balls.

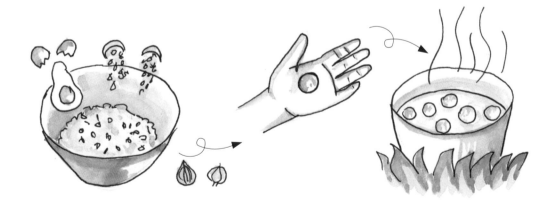

Potato Gratin

Makes 3–5 portions

Vegetable oil as needed

100 g garlic, peeled and minced

10 g thyme, roughly chopped

1 litre cooking cream

12–15 medium Russet or Holland
  potatoes, peeled

2 Tbsp ground white pepper

2 Tbsp salt

250 g mozzarella, shredded

Preheat oven to 180°C. Prepare a deep baking dish with at least 7.5-cm (3-inch) tall sides.

In a pot, heat oil over low heat and fry garlic and thyme until fragrant. Add cream and bring to a simmer, then remove from heat. Set aside.

Slice potatoes, preferably with a mandolin, into 0.5-cm thick slices. Add potatoes into the cream as you slice to prevent slices from browning through oxidation.

Return pot with cream and potatoes to a low heat. Stir gently and constantly to prevent potato slices from burning at the bottom of the pot. Cook for 15 minutes until cream starts to reduce and the potatoes are half-cooked. A half-cooked potato slice should still be firm but not hard and raw-tasting.

Season with pepper and salt, adjusting according to taste.

Arrange potato slices evenly in prepared baking dish. Gently press each potato slice down to pack a snug layer of slices. Pour cream over each completed layer before arranging the next layer.

Bake for 15–18 minutes until golden brown. Remove the dish from the oven and leave to rest for 30 minutes. Keep oven heated at 180°C.

Top dish with mozzarella, making sure to cover the surface evenly. Bake until mozzarella melts and turns golden brown, rotating and checking on the dish every 5 minutes.

Serve hot. This can keep refrigerated for a week. Reheat using a microwave.

Also known as gratin dauphinoise, this is a typical dish from southern France. I wasn't really a big fan of potatoes, unless they were cooked in chicken curry or served as fries. But this creamy, cheesy baked potato dish won me over. When I first had it, I fell in love with it! As it turns out, many people are fans of this as well.

One Chinese festival that I enjoy celebrating is Dragon Boat Festival. I must admit, what I like most about it is being able to eat my mum's homemade *chang* (rice dumplings). There are two types I like very much, and this is one of them (I'm sharing the other *chang* recipe in this book on page 106). It is usually paired with sugar or sweet condiments like *kaya* (coconut jam, page 47) and eaten as a dessert. As rice can be quite filling, I sometimes have it for breakfast or lunch!

Kee Chang

Makes 10–15 rice dumplings

1 kg glutinous rice

2 g alkaline water

1 packet dried bamboo leaves, soaked overnight to soften

Reed string for tying, soaked overnight to soften (substitute with hemp string or cooking twine)

50 g sugar

In a large pot, soak rice overnight or at least 8 hours.

Drain rice, then stir in alkaline water until rice is evenly yellow.

To wrap a dumpling, stack a bamboo leaf on top of another, then fold both short edges of the leaves together, overlapping them to form a cone. It should be large enough to fit in your palm.

Fill cone with rice until nearly full and pack rice in gently with the back of a spoon. Wrap bamboo leaves around the rice to seal dumpling and form a pyramid. Secure leaves in place with reed string, but do not tie it too tightly, as the rice will expand as it cooks.

Bring a large pot of water to a boil. When water is boiling, submerge dumplings and adjust to medium heat. Cover and boil dumplings for 3 hours, checking the water level occasionally. Top up pot with more hot water to make sure dumplings are fully covered.

Remove from heat and hang dumplings to dry until bamboo leaves are dry to the touch.

Serve with sugar on the side. You can also serve this with *gula melaka* (palm sugar) syrup or *kaya*.

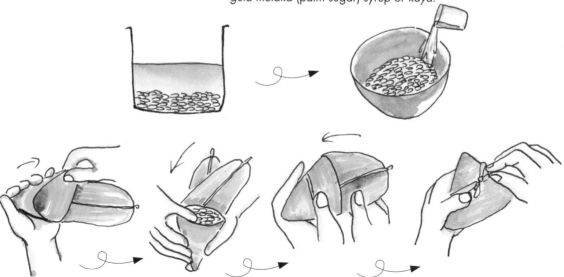

Kaya

Makes 450–900 ml

1 bunch pandan leaves,
   about 100 g

50 ml water

12 eggs

500 g sugar

40 ml coconut milk

Chop pandan leaves and place in a food processor. Add water and blend together. Strain pandan mixture through a muslin cloth or fine strainer, squeezing to extract as much liquid as possible. Refrigerate pandan extract to chill.

In a large heatproof bowl, whisk eggs and sugar until combined, then add coconut milk and pandan extract.

Fill a pot halfway with water and bring to a boil. Sit egg mixture over the pot and adjust heat to medium. Using a spatula, stir continuously while heating mixture for about an hour, until mixture is thick and smooth.

Remove from heat and leave to cool completely before transferring to a jar. This can be kept for 1 month refrigerated.

Enjoy with *kee chang* or spread on toast.

Kaya is a coconut jam that's popular in Singapore, Malaysia, Indonesia and other Southeast Asian places. It's creamy, sweet and often spread on breakfast toast — it also goes well with soft dinner rolls (page 14). My mum made *kaya* to go with her *kee chang* (alkaline rice dumplings, page 45), and the extra would be saved for having at breakfast. Although cooking it takes a little bit of effort (as you have to watch and stir it constantly), it's very satisfying to taste the *kaya* you've made.

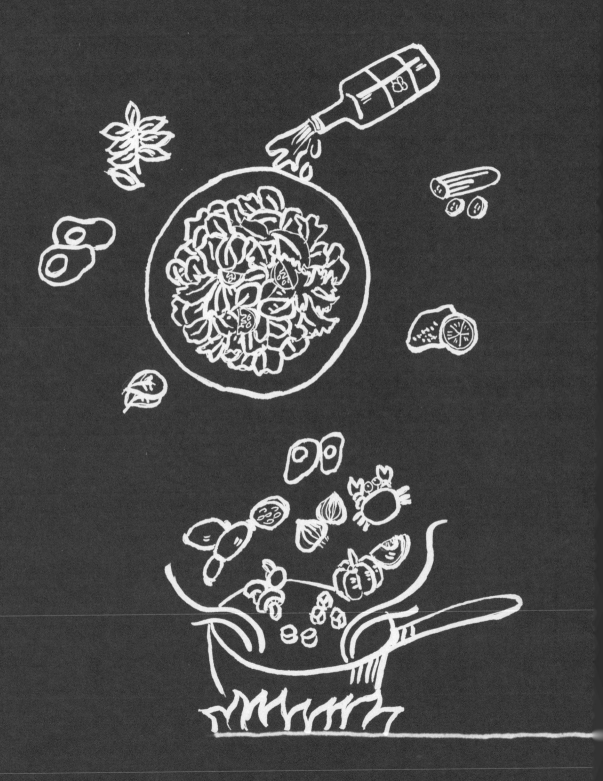

Creamy Shiitake Mushroom Soup   50

Creamy Spinach Soup   53

Pumpkin Soup   54

French Onion Soup   57

Minestrone Soup   58

Chinese Spinach and Egg Soup with Goji Berries   61

Pork Rib Soup with Lotus Root   62

Ginger Fish Soup with XO   65

Crab Meat and Egg White Soup   66

Laksa Salad   69

Shredded Chicken Salad with Asian Dressing   70

Caesar Salad with Homemade Mayonnaise   73

SALADS AND SOUPS

Creamy Shiitake Mushroom Soup

Makes 4–6 portions

2 Tbsp olive oil

20 g garlic, peeled and sliced

1 yellow onion, peeled and sliced

400 g shiitake mushrooms, sliced

50 ml milk

250 ml cooking cream + more
to taste

1.2 litres chicken / vegetable
stock or water

2 tsp sugar

2 Tbsp salt, or to taste

1 tsp ground white pepper, or to
taste

125 ml water

3 Tbsp all-purpose flour

In a large pot, heat oil over medium heat and fry garlic and onion until lightly browned. Add mushrooms and cook until softened. Add milk, 125 ml cream, 600 ml stock, then bring to a boil and simmer for 15–20 minutes.

Remove mixture from heat and leave to cool for 30 minutes before blending until smooth. Strain into a pot, return to heat and add the remaining cream and stock. When soup comes to a boil, whisk until it is well combined. Simmer for 15 minutes.

Remove from heat and stir in sugar. Adjust seasoning with salt and pepper according to taste. It is best to use the quantities listed as a guide, adding salt and pepper gradually, and tasting after each addition. This way, you will not over-season the soup.

In a bowl, combine water and flour, mixing well to form a slurry. Pour slurry into soup through a strainer, stirring constantly. If you prefer a thinner consistency, add less slurry.

Taste and adjust seasoning to taste with more salt or cream. Serve hot with soft dinner rolls.

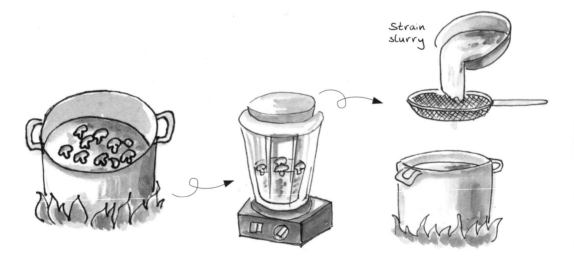

Strain slurry

I learnt to make this soup while I was working in a restaurant that served Western cuisine. This is not a bland creamy soup with some mushroom slices that you get in canned soup — it has a rich mushroom flavour and goes really well with soft dinner rolls (page 14).

Even though my siblings and I did not enjoy eating vegetables, we would pester our mum to cook spinach when we were children. We had watched 'Popeye the Sailor' cartoons, and those made us think that eating spinach would make us strong and powerful! Thanks to Popeye, and our mum's cooking, we got lots of vitamins, minerals and fibre from spinach. This soup is a good way to help picky eaters (like your child or even yourself) eat more vegetables.

Creamy Spinach Soup

Makes 4–6 portions

2 Tbsp olive oil

20 g garlic, peeled and sliced

1 yellow onion, peeled and sliced

50 ml milk

250 ml cooking cream + more
   to taste

1.2 litres chicken / vegetable
   stock or water

400 g spinach, chopped

2 tsp sugar

2 Tbsp salt, or to taste

1 tsp ground white pepper,
   or to taste

125 ml water

3 Tbsp all-purpose flour

In a large pot, heat oil over medium heat and fry garlic
and onion until lightly browned. Add milk, 125 ml cream
and 600 ml stock, followed by spinach. Bring to a boil and
simmer for 10–15 minutes.

Remove mixture from heat and leave to cool for 30 minutes
before blending until smooth. Strain into a pot, return to
heat and add the remaining cream and stock. When soup
comes to a boil, whisk until it is well combined. Simmer for
10 minutes.

Remove from heat and stir in sugar. Adjust seasoning
with salt and pepper according to taste. It is best to use
the quantities listed as a guide, adding salt and pepper
gradually, and tasting after each addition. This way, you will
not over-season the soup.

In a bowl, combine water and flour, mixing well to form
a slurry. Pour slurry into soup through a strainer, stirring
constantly. If you prefer a thinner consistency, add less slurry.

Taste and adjust seasoning to taste with more salt or cream.
Serve hot.

Strain slurry

Pumpkin Soup

Makes 4–6 portions

2 Tbsp olive oil

1 yellow onion, peeled and sliced

1 pumpkin, about 2–3 kg,
   peeled and cut into cubes

1 carrot, peeled and cut
   into chunks

2 Tbsp sugar

100 ml milk

200 ml cooking cream + more
   to taste

1.2 litres chicken / vegetable
   stock or water

1 tsp salt, or to taste

125 ml water (optional)

3 Tbsp all-purpose flour (optional)

In a large pot, heat oil over medium heat and fry onion until lightly browned. Add pumpkin, carrot and sugar, frying until pumpkin is lightly browned. Add milk, 100 ml cream and 600 ml stock. Bring to a boil and simmer for 15–20 minutes.

Remove mixture from heat and leave to cool for 30 minutes before blending until smooth. Strain into a pot, return to heat and add the remaining cream and stock. When soup comes to a boil, whisk until it is well combined. Simmer for 15 minutes.

Remove from heat and stir in salt. Adjust seasoning with more salt and sugar according to taste. It is best to add more salt and sugar gradually, tasting after each addition. This way, you will not over-season the soup.

In a bowl, combine water and flour, mixing well to form a slurry. Pour slurry into soup through a strainer, stirring constantly. If you find the soup's consistency already to your liking, feel free to omit this step.

Serve hot.

Cream & milk

When I was learning to cook Western-style cuisine, I was really confused by this soup! A pumpkin tastes sweet, and soups are usually savoury. As a junior staff member in the kitchen, I asked my chef for advice on this stumbling point. He wisely said, "All ingredients have their unique flavours, and it's our job as chefs to enhance these flavours rather than hide them with others. Don't try to make the ingredient taste different; make it taste better." Instead of running from the sweetness of the pumpkin, I've decided to showcase it. I have to thank this soup for helping me understand an important philosophy of cooking.

French onion soup changed my view of onions. Onions are usually not the star of a dish, always taking on a supporting role in stir-fries, soups and curries. In this soup, sweet and savoury are combined in a such a delightful way. One great thing about this soup is that nothing will go to waste. You can use wine that's leftover from an opened bottle to add to the soup. And if you have leftover soup, you can blend it to make a red wine sauce for grilled steak or chicken.

French Onion Soup

Makes 4–6 portions

2 Tbsp olive oil

20 g garlic, peeled and smashed

15 g thyme

6 big yellow onions, peeled and sliced

4 Tbsp sugar

350 ml cooking red wine

1.2 litres stock (chicken / beef / vegetable)

Ground black pepper to taste

Salt to taste

$^1/_2$ French loaf

10 g mozzarella, grated

In a large pot, heat oil over medium heat and add garlic, thyme and onions. Fry until onions are lightly browned before stirring in sugar.

Sauté onions a little further until they turn a caramel brown. Gradually stir in wine and cook for 5 minutes until mixture is reduced.

Add stock and bring to a boil. Reduce to low heat and simmer for 20–30 minutes. Adjust seasoning with salt and pepper to taste.

While soup is simmering, cut bread into 6 slices and toast in a toaster oven.

Ladle soup into individual serving bowls, then top each bowl with a bread slice and sprinkle with mozzarella. Serve immediately.

Red wine

Crouton with melted cheese

Minestrone Soup

Makes 4 portions

2 Tbsp olive oil

1 head garlic, peeled
   and smashed

1 onion, peeled and diced

1 carrot, peeled and diced

2 potatoes, peeled and diced

4 stalks celery, diced

4 tomatoes, diced

100 g shiitake mushrooms, diced

1 Tbsp sugar

100 g tomato paste

1.5 litres chicken / vegetable
   stock or water

3 bay leaves

2 tsp salt

2 tsp ground white pepper

In a large saucepan, heat oil over medium heat and fry garlic and onion until fragrant. Add diced carrot, potatoes, celery, tomatoes and mushrooms, as well as sugar, then fry until lightly browned. (Dice any leftover vegetables you don't want to waste and add them in at this stage too.)

Add in tomato paste and sauté vegetables until softened.

Add stock and bay leaves. Bring to a boil and let simmer for 20 minutes.

Adjust seasoning with salt and pepper. Serve immediately.

Bay leaves

Stock

I call this "soup for lazy people". It is super easy to prepare and really yummy. If you don't have any stock on hand, just use water for its base. This soup is also perfect for busy people. It is great for using up any leftover vegetables you have (saving your money from being wasted), and it can keep for a week in the fridge (saving your energy and food prep time). The extra soup can be heated up and freshened with more vegetables or meat if you like. The classic way to have this soup is with pasta (either boiled separately or in the soup itself), but it also works with ramen noodles, even the ones from a cup! Alternatively, you can have it with bread.

My mum used to cook this soup often for my siblings and I when we were young. She said that this soup would help us grow tall and strong, and have bright eyes so that we could study well. We didn't think much of it back then, but I later realised she was probably right. Both spinach and goji berries are full of vitamins A and C, which are good for eye health.

Chinese Spinach and Egg Soup with Goji Berries

Makes 4–6 portions

2 Tbsp vegetable oil

20 g garlic, peeled and smashed

20 g dried prawns

1.2 litres water or stock (chicken / pork / vegetable)

2 tsp salt

1 Tbsp sugar

15 g goji berries (wolfberries)

200 g spinach

2 eggs

1 tsp ground white pepper

In a large saucepan, heat oil over medium heat and fry garlic and dried prawns until lightly browned and fragrant. Add stock and bring to a boil. Simmer for 15 minutes.

Adjust seasoning with salt and sugar.

Add goji berries and bring to a boil again. When soup is boiling, add spinach and cook until wilted, which should take no more than 5 minutes.

Adjust heat to low. Crack eggs one at a time into the soup. Do not stir the soup, so that the eggs are not broken up as they cook.

After 1 minute, when eggs are almost cooked, turn off the heat. Season soup with pepper and serve hot.

Pork Rib Soup with Lotus Root

Makes 4–6 portions

2 Tbsp vegetable oil

2 heads garlic, peeled and smashed

500–600 g pork ribs

$^1/_2$ cup Shaoxing wine

600 g lotus root, scrubbed clean, peeled and sliced into 0.5- to 1-cm thick slices

100 g dried shiitake mushrooms, soaked in water for 15 minutes

150 g peanuts, soaked in hot water overnight

3 Tbsp light soy sauce + more to taste

15 g goji berries (wolfberries)

2.5 litres pork / chicken stock

2 Tbsp sugar

3–4 tsp salt

In a wok, heat oil over high heat. Fry garlic and pork ribs until ribs are lightly browned. Drizzle in Shaoxing wine and stir in as it sizzles. Remove from heat.

In a large pot, place pork ribs with lotus root and drained mushrooms and peanuts. Pour soy sauce over, then add goji berries followed by stock. Bring to a boil over high heat, then reduce heat to low and leave to simmer for at least 1 hour 30 minutes.

Adjust seasoning with sugar and salt to taste. Add more soy sauce if it's to your liking. Cook for another 15 minutes, then remove from heat and serve hot.

If you have a slow cooker, you can also use it to prepare this soup using this fuss-free method, especially if you are out for the day at work. Place all the ingredients, except sugar and salt, in the slow cooker pot. Set the slow cooker to auto. Before serving soup, season with sugar and salt to taste.

For the Cantonese, soup is a must-have at dinner. This is one of the most popular and well-known Cantonese soups. I think it's because it's so easy to prepare. Now, with the help of slow cookers, it's made even easier for busy people to prepare. I've provided both methods of preparing this soup, but I recommend trying to cook this soup over the stove at least once. My favourite part of making this soup is listening to the sizzle of Shaoxing wine in the wok and smelling the aroma of garlic, pork and wine wafting through the kitchen.

Without fail, the food stall with a queue at any hawker centre would be one that sells fish soup. I think this is because people are becoming more conscious of their health, and fish soup is one of the few dishes found at a hawker centre that is quite light and nutritious. Because this dish is pretty easy to make at home, I prefer to do so rather than eat this from a hawker stall. You can add more vegetables and reduce the salt, sugar and oil according to your preference.

Ginger Fish Soup with XO

Makes 4–6 portions

500–600 g whole white fish, deboned (buy a whole fish and ask the fishmonger to debone it for you, and keep the head and bones for this soup), or frozen white fish fillet (purchase fish bones for stock separately at supermarkets or wet markets)

4 tsp salt + more to taste

$^1/_2$ tsp ground white pepper + more to taste

2 tsp sesame oil + more for garnishing

1 Tbsp vegetable oil

30 g ginger, peeled and smashed

20 g garlic, peeled and smashed

5 Tbsp Shaoxing wine

1.8 litres chicken / vegetable stock or water

1 sprig coriander + more for garnishing

40 g rock sugar

2 Tbsp fish sauce

6 tomatoes, cut into wedges

300 g Chinese cabbage

300 g silken tofu, cubed

1 stalk spring onion, chopped

Slice fish fillet and place in a bowl. Rub with salt, pepper and sesame oil, then cover and refrigerate while cooking the soup.

In a large pot, heat oil over medium heat. Fry smashed ginger and garlic until fragrant. Add fish bones and head and fry until fish head is cooked through, then deglaze the pot by drizzling in Shaoxing wine.

Add stock, coriander, rock sugar and fish sauce. Bring to a boil and simmer for 20 minutes.

Adjust seasoning with salt and pepper. Add more wine, if the flavour is to your liking. Add tomatoes and Chinese cabbage, then boil for another 10 minutes.

To serve, poach fish slices in the boiling soup briefly until cooked through, about 1 minute. Divide tofu cubes into serving bowls, then portion out fish slices and vegetables before ladling soup over.

Top with spring onion and chopped coriander leaves. Drizzle with a little sesame oil and serve with rice or noodles.

Crab Meat and Egg White Soup

Makes 3–5 portions

1.5 litres chicken stock

250–300 g chicken breast

150–200 g crab meat (available frozen or canned)

140 ml Shaoxing wine

2 Tbsp sugar

3 tsp salt

1 tsp ground white pepper

30–40 g potato starch

5 egg whites, lightly beaten

In a pot, bring chicken stock to a boil. When stock is boiling, add chicken, adjust heat to low and simmer for 15 minutes. Turn off the heat, remove chicken and plunge in a bowl of iced water to cool. Shred cooled chicken and set aside.

Return stock to heat and bring to a boil again. Add crab meat and simmer for 15 minutes to impart crab flavour to soup and cook crab meat.

Add shredded chicken and Shaoxing wine, then boil for 10 minutes.

Adjust seasoning with sugar, salt and pepper. Combine potato starch with water to form a slurry that's easy to stir. Add slurry gradually to soup, stirring continuously, until soup is slightly thickened.

Turn off the heat and pour in egg whites gradually, stirring the soup and letting the residual heat cook the egg whites.

If you prefer, add a few more drops of Shaoxing wine or brandy — this will give the soup an extra kick in flavour. Serve hot with pepper and black vinegar as condiments.

Shredded chicken
Crab meat
Slurry
Egg whites

Shark's fin soup is a dish usually served at special occasions, like a Chinese wedding banquet. And so it's a dish that many don't think of as something easy to cook at home. Well, this soup tastes exactly like shark's fin soup, except it doesn't need shark's fin at all, and it can be made at home. It has potato starch to thank for its smooth and luxuriously thick texture, and crab meat and Shaoxing wine for how savoury it is.

Laksa is one of my favourite Singaporean dishes. Before I understood Singapore's cuisine better, I thought that it lacked strong and heavy flavours that I grew up with in Malaysia. When I tried laksa in Singapore for the first time, I realised there was a lot more to the food in this country than I knew of. This salad draws inspiration from the fragant and rich flavours of laksa, and it's so easy to make.

Laksa Salad

Makes 2–3 portions

700 g romaine lettuce, washed

5–6 *tau pok* (deep-fried beancurd puff), deep-fried until crispy

12–15 prawns, boiled and peeled

4–5 eggs, hard-boiled, peeled and cut into wedges

15 g dried prawns, fried with olive oil until crispy

10 g laksa leaves, finely chopped

Curry powder for garnishing

LAKSA SAUCE

4 eggs

4 tsp coconut oil

A pinch of salt

Ground black pepper to taste

4 tsp coconut milk powder

1 tsp curry powder

50 g laksa leaves

Prepare laksa sauce. In a bowl, beat eggs lightly, then gradually add oil, whisking constantly to emulsify oil and eggs. Season with salt and pepper, then whisk until mixture is thick. Its consistency should resemble that of mayonnaise.

Add coconut milk powder, curry powder and laksa leaves. Mix to combine, cover and set aside until needed.

Tear lettuce leaves into desired size and place in a large bowl. Add *tau pok*, then pour laksa sauce over. Toss to coat lettuce and *tau pok* evenly.

Dish out onto serving plates and top with prawns, eggs and crispy dried prawns. Sprinkle laksa leaves and curry powder over salad.

Shredded Chicken Salad with Asian Dressing

Makes 2 portions

150–180 g chicken breast

200 g salad greens of your choice, such as a mesclun mix or romaine lettuce

10 slices Japanese cucumber

10 cherry tomatoes

10 g sesame seeds

DRESSING

150 ml olive oil

2 tsp sesame oil

4 tsp balsamic vinegar

1 Tbsp light soy sauce

2 Tbsp oyster sauce

Prepare dressing. Place all ingredients in a squeeze bottle or vinaigrette bottle. Shake well to mix. Set aside until needed.

Bring a pot of water to a boil. Add chicken and adjust heat to low. Simmer for 15 minutes before removing chicken and plunging in a bowl of cold water to cool. Drain and shred cooled chicken.

Divide salad greens, cucumber slices and cherry tomatoes between 2 bowls. Top with shredded chicken.

Pour sauce over salad and sprinkle with sesame seeds. Serves as a side accompanying dishes such as roast spring chicken (page 91) or lemon and white wine baked fish (page 92).

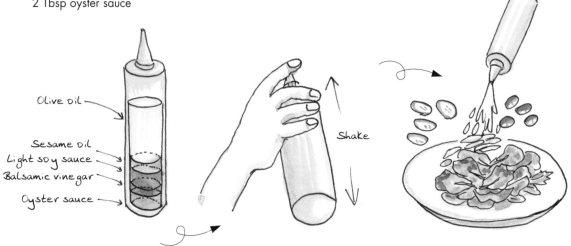

Olive oil

Sesame oil
Light soy sauce
Balsamic vinegar
Oyster sauce

Shake

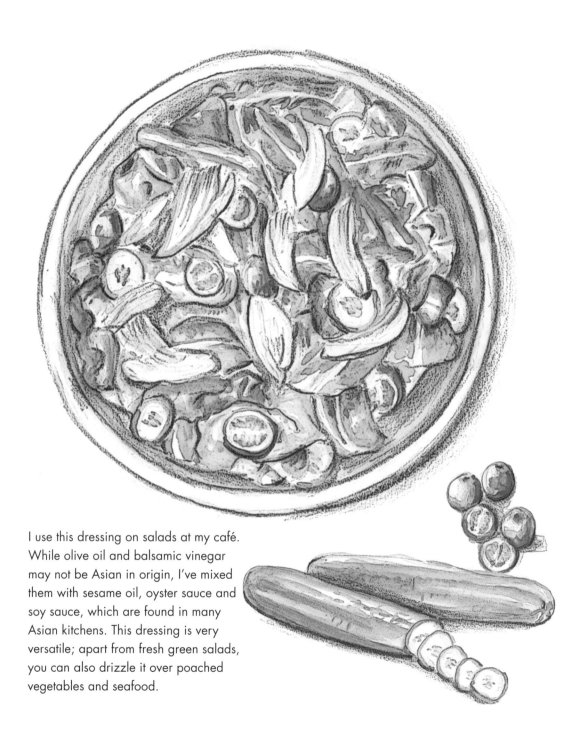

I use this dressing on salads at my café. While olive oil and balsamic vinegar may not be Asian in origin, I've mixed them with sesame oil, oyster sauce and soy sauce, which are found in many Asian kitchens. This dressing is very versatile; apart from fresh green salads, you can also drizzle it over poached vegetables and seafood.

Caesar salad is a standard restaurant salad, which makes it easy to overlook or treat as a boring dish. It's actually a salad that has a wonderful combination of textures, from crispy croutons and salty bacon bits, to crunchy lettuce leaves coated with creamy mayonnaise. I've always liked this salad as it feels like I'm having a fresh, more indulgent version of vegetable chips. The mayonnaise can be kept for a week in the fridge, and it can be mixed with sliced apples and cucumber, then topped with toasted sliced nuts to make a refreshing treat.

Caesar Salad with Homemade Mayonnaise

Makes 2 portions

200 g romaine lettuce

4 strips bacon

10 g Parmesan cheese

$^1/_2$ lemon, cut into wedges

CROUTONS

1 French loaf

2 Tbsp olive oil

10 g Italian (flat-leaf) parsley, finely chopped

1 Tbsp minced garlic

MAYONNAISE

2 egg yolks

2 tsp Dijon mustard

1 tsp minced garlic

Juice from $^1/_2$ lemon

200 ml olive oil

Oil from bacon (see method)

Salt to taste

Ground black pepper to taste

Prepare croutons. Preheat the oven to 200°C. Slice bread into cubes and place in a bowl. Add olive oil, parsley and garlic, then toss gently to coat bread cubes evenly. Spread on a baking tray and toast for 5–6 minutes until crispy. Leave to cool.

Prepare salad. Tear romaine lettuce leaves into desired size and place in a large bowl.

Lay bacon strips on a wire rack and place on a rimmed baking tray in the oven. Bake at 200°C for 12–15 minutes until crispy. Reserve bacon oil for mayonnaise and leave bacon to cool. Crush cooled bacon into fine bits.

Prepare mayonnaise. Place egg yolks, Dijon mustard, garlic, and lemon juice in a mixing bowl and whisk to combine. Gradually add olive oil and bacon oil, whisking continuously to emulsify oils in mixture, until a mayonnaise-like consistency is achieved. Season with salt and pepper to taste.

To assemble salad, add mayonnaise to lettuce and toss gently to coat lettuce evenly. Portion onto serving plates, then top with croutons, crispy bacon bits and shaved Parmesan. Garnish with lemon wedges.

Steamed Eggs with Pickled Vegetables and Minced Meat   76

Steamed Eggs with Miso and Tofu   79

Teochew-style Steamed Fish   80

Hakka-style Steamed Fish   83

Sichuan Poached Fish with Pickled Mustard Greens   84

Crispy Rice Risotto with White Wine Sauce   87

Potstick Chicken Rice   88

Roast Spring Chicken   91

Lemon and White Wine Baked Fish   92

Home-style Cereal Prawns   95

Ketchup Prawns   96

Pasta Vongole with White Wine Sauce   99

Aglio Olio Laksa Pasta   100

Seafood Paella   103

Samsui Chicken   104

Cantonese Bak Chang   106

EASY DISHES FOR A SMALL FAMILY

Steamed Eggs with Pickled Vegetables and Minced Meat

Makes 2–3 portions served with rice

60 g chicken or pork, minced

30 g mushrooms, diced

30 g *dong choi* (Tianjin preserved cabbage), soaked in water for 15 minutes to remove salt

1 Tbsp oyster sauce

4 tsp light soy sauce

1 Tbsp vegetable oil

2 tsp salt + more to taste

1 tsp sugar

7 eggs

300 g silken tofu, cut into cubes

700 ml chicken stock or water

1 stalk spring onion, thinly sliced

1 tsp sesame oil

In a bowl, place meat, mushrooms, *dong choi*, both sauces, oil, salt and sugar. Mix well and leave to marinate.

Crack eggs into a large bowl and beat well. Add marinated mixture to eggs and mix well. The ratio of this mixture to the stock or water should be 1:2.

Arrange silken tofu evenly on a steaming tray. Pour egg mixture over tofu, followed by chicken stock. Sprinkle with a pinch of salt. Leave for 15 minutes to let bubbles dissipate, or use a spoon to remove bubbles.

To cook egg mixture in a rice cooker, prepare rice as you would normally. Add water to rice cooker pot, then place steaming rack over rice. Place steaming tray with egg mixture on top and follow regular setting to cook rice.

To cook egg mixture over the stove, fill wok with water for steaming and insert a steaming rack. Bring water to a boil. When water is boiling, place steaming tray with egg mixture on top of rack. Cover, adjust heat to medium and steam for 20 minutes.

Garnish with spring onion and sesame oil. Serve hot.

This dish is one of many healthy and delicious steamed dishes you can prepare in an electric rice cooker. I learnt this easy way of preparing dishes from my mother. She would wake up at 6 a.m. to prepare this dish on days she needed to help my dad out at the farm and wouldn't be home to prepare lunch for my brother and I. She would put the prepared egg mixture in the refrigerator before leaving the house, and all I had to do was let it steam in the rice cooker while the rice was cooking.

This dish is vegetarian, which makes it perfect for when you don't feel like having a heavy protein side dish. It also only takes 20 minutes to prepare (apart from cooking time). You can make use of a steaming rack in a rice cooker to steam this dish while you are cooking the rice. It makes cleaning up easy as well.

Steamed Eggs with Miso and Tofu

Makes 2–3 portions served with rice

4 Tbsp miso paste

40 g carrots, diced

20 g shiitake mushrooms, diced

2 Tbsp oyster sauce

1 Tbsp light soy sauce

1 Tbsp vegetable oil

2 tsp salt + more to taste

1 tsp sugar

7 eggs

300 g silken tofu, cut into cubes

700 ml water

1 stalk spring onion, thinly sliced

1 tsp sesame oil

In a bowl, place miso paste, carrot, mushrooms, both sauces, oil, salt and sugar. Mix well and leave to marinate.

Crack eggs into a large bowl and beat well. Add marinated mixture to eggs and mix well. The ratio of this mixture to the water added later should be 1:2.

Arrange tofu cubes evenly on a steaming tray. Pour egg mixture over tofu, followed by 700 ml water. Season with a pinch of salt. Leave for 15 minutes to let bubbles dissipate, or use a spoon to remove bubbles.

To cook egg mixture in a rice cooker, prepare rice as you would normally. Add water for cooking rice to rice cooker pot, then place steaming rack over rice. Place steaming tray with egg mixture on top and use the regular setting for cooking rice.

To cook egg mixture over the stove, fill wok with water for steaming and insert a steaming rack. Bring water to a boil. When water is boiling, place steaming tray with egg mixture on top of rack. Cover, adjust heat to medium and steam for 20 minutes.

Garnish with spring onion and sesame oil. Serve hot.

Teochew-style Steamed Fish

Makes 2–3 portions served with rice

500 g whole white fish (sea bass / barramundi / grouper), deboned

1 tsp salt + more to taste

2 tsp ground white pepper + more to taste

2 tsp sesame oil + more for garnishing

1 tsp vegetable oil

3–4 cloves garlic, peeled and smashed

4 slices peeled ginger

100 g *kiam chye* (preserved mustard greens), sliced

2 sour plums, stones removed, mashed

3 Tbsp Shaoxing wine

100 ml chicken stock or water

1 Tbsp sugar

3 tomatoes, cut into wedges

150 g silken tofu, cut into cubes

150 g cabbage, leaves cut into large squares

2 red chillies, sliced

50 g shiitake mushrooms, sliced

1 stalk spring onion, sliced

1 sprig coriander, chopped

Rub fish with salt, pepper and sesame oil. Place on a steaming tray, cover with cling film or foil and leave to marinate in the refrigerator.

In a medium saucepan, heat vegetable oil and fry garlic over medium heat until fragrant. Add ginger and *kiam chye*, frying them lightly. Add sour plums, Shaoxing wine and stock. Bring to a boil and simmer for 10 minutes.

Remove from heat and adjust seasoning with sugar, salt and pepper according to taste.

Arrange tomatoes and tofu around fish, then cover with cabbage, chillies and mushrooms. Pour sauce over fish and vegetables.

To cook fish in a rice cooker, prepare rice as you would normally. Add water to rice cooker pot, then place steaming rack over rice. Place steaming tray with fish on top and follow regular setting to cook rice.

To cook fish over the stove, fill wok with water for steaming and insert a steaming rack. Bring water to a boil. When water is boiling, place steaming tray with fish on top of rack. Cover, adjust heat to medium and steam for 15–18 minutes.

Garnish with spring onion and coriander. If desired, drizzle with a few drops of sesame oil.

As my mum is Hakka and my dad is Cantonese, we usually ate dishes from those two cuisines at home. Thus, I remember vividly the first time I tasted Teochew-style steamed fish. My dad had come home with a fresh grouper from the neighbouring farm. We rarely had a whole fish brought home, so my mum decided to cook it in a different style. The salted vegetables and sour plum brought out the natural sweetness of the fish, and the combination of flavours amazed me.

This is one of my favourites dishes by my mum. In fact, I'm not particularly fond of eating fish because of the trouble of picking out the bones. But when my mum cooks this dish, I would be the first at the table.

Hakka-style Steamed Fish

Makes 2–3 portions served with rice

500–600 g white fish (sea bass /
  barramundi / grouper),
  deboned

1 tsp salt + more to taste

1 tsp ground white pepper
  + more to taste

2 Tbsp vegetable oil

10 cloves garlic, peeled and
  finely chopped

1 large yellow onion, peeled and
  finely chopped

2 Tbsp *tau cheo* (fermented soy
  bean paste)

15 g ginger, peeled and
  finely chopped

2 red chillies, finely chopped

2 Tbsp oyster sauce

3 Tbsp Shaoxing wine

250 ml chicken stock or water

2 Tbsp sugar

1 Tbsp light soy sauce

20 g shiitake mushrooms, stems
  removed, sliced

1 stalk spring onion, sliced

1 sprig coriander, chopped

Sesame oil for garnishing

Butterfly the fish by slicing it horizontally, keeping both halves attached on one end. Marinate with salt and pepper, then place on a steaming tray. Cover and leave in the refrigerator.

In a medium saucepan, heat oil and add garlic, onion, *tau cheo*, and half of the ginger and chillies. Fry lightly for 5 minutes before adding oyster sauce and Shaoxing wine. When mixture is fragrant, add stock, bring to a boil and simmer for 5 minutes.

Remove from heat and adjust seasoning with sugar, salt and pepper according to taste.

Pour sauce over fish, add soy sauce, then top with mushrooms and the remaining ginger and chilli.

To cook fish in a rice cooker, prepare rice as you would normally. Add water to rice cooker pot, then place steaming rack over rice. Place steaming tray with fish on top and follow regular setting to cook rice.

To cook fish over the stove, fill wok with water for steaming and insert a steaming rack. Bring water to a boil. When water is boiling, place steaming tray with fish on top of rack. Cover, adjust heat to medium and steam for 15–20 minutes.

Garnish with spring onion and coriander. If desired, drizzle with a few drops of sesame oil.

Sichuan Poached Fish with Pickled Mustard Greens

Makes 2–3 portions served with rice

500–600 g white fish (sea bass / barramundi / grouper)

1 tsp + 4 tsp salt

1 tsp ground white pepper

1 egg

2 Tbsp potato starch

8 Tbsp vegetable oil

6 slices peeled ginger

250 ml Shaoxing wine

1.2 litres chicken stock or water

8 cloves garlic, left unpeeled and smashed

4 red chillies, diced

6 dried chillies, diced

2 onions, peeled and sliced

250 g *kiam chye* (preserved mustard greens), sliced

300 g silken tofu, cut into cubes

2 Tbsp fish sauce

1 Tbsp sugar

1 Tbsp Sichuan peppercorns

2 stalks spring onion, chopped

Debone fish and slice into 4 x 4-cm slices. Reserve fish bones. If you are unsure of how to debone a fish, you can request the fishmonger to debone it for you. Place fish slices in a bowl and add 1 tsp salt, pepper, egg and potato starch. Mix well and leave to marinate.

In a pot over medium heat, add 1 Tbsp oil and fry reserved fish bones with 3 ginger slices until fragrant. Add 125 ml Shaoxing wine and bring to a simmer before adding stock. Simmer for 15–20 minutes, then strain and set aside stock.

In a separate pot over medium heat, add 2 Tbsp oil and fry 4 cloves garlic, the remaining ginger slices, 2 red chillies, 3 dried chillies and onions until fragrant. Add *kiam chye* and tofu, frying lightly for 5 minutes until fragrant. Add the remaining Shaoxing wine and reserved stock. Bring to a boil and simmer for 15 minutes. Season with fish sauce, sugar and 4 tsp salt.

Poach fish slices in simmering soup. This should take about a minute. Remove from heat and portion fish slices into serving bowls. Ladle soup into bowls.

Heat 5 Tbsp oil in a frying pan over low heat. Add the remaining garlic, red chillies and dried chillies, followed by peppercorns. Sauté until the oil turns red. Drizzle chilli oil over fish soup and garnish with spring onion.

84

Sichuan food has become really popular, probably because of its strong flavours. I tried this dish at a famous Sichuan restaurant in Singapore, and it immediately reminded me of *tau cheo* steamed fish that's made with a lot more spices. I loved the flavours but found the dish a little too oily and the fish meat too mushy. My version tries to improve on these points.

This is a favourite on the menu at my café, but I didn't come up with the idea for it while developing and testing dishes for the menu. We had been running for about four years when one day, two American tourists walked in for dinner. They were craving risotto but we didn't have any. I told them I would whip up something inspired by risotto and came out with this dish shortly after that. They loved the dish so much that I tried serving it to other customers subsequently. It's been on the café's menu ever since. We typically use seafood, but if you prefer, you can make this with store-bought crispy roasted pork belly (about 150 g).

Crispy Rice Risotto with White Wine Sauce

Makes 2 portions

6 Tbsp vegetable oil

2 cups freshly cooked
long-grain rice

3 cloves garlic, peeled
and minced

$^1/_2$ broccoli, diced

$^1/_2$ carrot, peeled and diced

6 button mushrooms, stems
removed, diced

4 prawns, peeled and shells
removed

4 scallops

6 mussels (frozen or fresh is fine)

8 tsp white wine

240 ml cooking cream

60 ml chicken stock or water

2 tsp chicken powder

1 tsp ground white pepper

3 tsp salt

2 sprigs English parsley,
finely chopped

A pinch of ground paprika

Heat a large frying pan until it starts to smoke, then add
4 Tbsp oil and adjust heat to low. Add rice to frying pan
and spread evenly, using a spatula to compress rice until rice
grains stick together and form an unbroken base. Pan-fry
rice on one side until crispy and brown, about 10 minutes.
Transfer crispy rice cake onto serving plate.

In a saucepan over medium heat, add 2 Tbsp oil and garlic,
then fry until fragrant. Add broccoli, carrot, mushrooms and
seafood, stir-frying until half-cooked before adding white
wine. When wine begins to evaporate, pour in cream and
stock. Simmer for 5 minutes.

Adjust seasoning with chicken powder, pepper and salt. You
may add more cream if you prefer a creamier sauce.

Ladle sauce over crispy rice cake and garnish with parsley
and paprika.

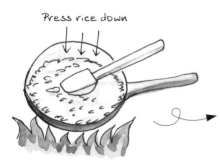

Press rice down

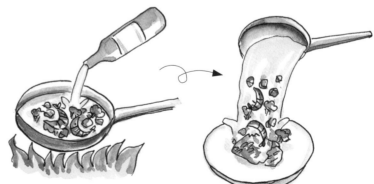

Potstick Chicken Rice

Makes 2 portions

6 cloves garlic, peeled and sliced
+ 10 g, peeled and minced

2 Tbsp oyster sauce

2 Tbsp dark soy sauce

1 Tbsp Shaoxing wine

500–600 g boneless chicken
thighs, fat trimmed and reserved

2 Tbsp vegetable oil + more for
deep-frying

20 g Chinese sausage, sliced

20 g *mui heong* (dried salted fish)

2 cups long grain rice, washed

2 tsp chicken powder

360 ml (2 rice cups) chicken stock
or water

100 g shiitake mushrooms, sliced

3 bok choy

4 Tbsp light soy sauce

1 Tbsp sesame oil

1 stalk spring onion, chopped

1 sprig coriander, chopped

Place sliced garlic, 1 Tbsp oyster sauce, 1 Tbsp dark soy
sauce and Shaoxing wine in a bowl. Add chicken and leave
to marinate for 15–30 minutes.

Heat 1 Tbsp vegetable oil in a frying pan over medium heat.
When oil is hot, place marinated chicken skin-side down.
Pan-fry until the skin is slightly charred. The chicken does not
need to be cooked through. Set aside.

To the same frying pan, add 1 Tbsp vegetable oil and lightly
pan-fry Chinese sausage for 1 minute. Set aside.

Heat enough oil for deep-frying in a pot over medium heat.
When oil is hot, deep-fry *mui heong* until crispy. Transfer onto
paper towels to absorb excess oil.

In a non-stick pot over medium heat, fry reserved chicken fat
with 5 g minced garlic until fragrant. Add rice and chicken
powder, then fry for 1 minute, stirring to mix well. Pour in
stock and bring to a boil. Adjust heat to medium-low and let
rice simmer as it cooks through.

When rice is nearly cooked (rice grains should be plump),
arrange chicken, mushroom, Chinese sausage, bok choy
and *mui heong* on top. Adjust heat to low, cover and cook
for 12 minutes until water is completely absorbed by rice.

In a bowl, mix the remaining minced garlic, oyster sauce
and dark soy sauce, light soy sauce and sesame oil together.
Drizzle mixture over rice and cook uncovered for another
5–6 minutes.

Garnish with spring onion and coriander. Serve hot.

Also known as claypot rice, this is usually offered mainly by specialised hawker stalls in Malaysia and Singapore. This is because it can't be prepared fully ahead of time, so hawkers take about 20–30 minutes to serve up an order. Waiting 30 minutes might seem tiresome when you're dining out, but the same amount of time used to whip up a meal at home is considered very reasonable. For your convenience, the chicken can be left to marinate overnight as well. With fluffy rice and a crispy bottom layer, this dish has a great mix of textures.

My mum used to cook a stewed chicken dish with
dried shiitake mushrooms and I loved the intensity
of the mushroom flavour. When I had roast chicken in Singapore for the first
time, it reminded me of that stew from my childhood because the meat was
tender and juicy. But I felt that something was missing — then I realised I was
so used to the flavour combination of dried shiitake mushrooms and chicken.
It made me long for my mum's cooking, so I had the idea of using a shiitake
mushroom rub on a roast chicken.

Roast Spring Chicken

Makes 2–3 portions

CHICKEN

10 g garlic, peeled and minced

50 g onion, peeled and minced

20 g dried shiitake mushrooms, processed into fine bits

5 g thyme, finely chopped

1 tsp ground black pepper

2 tsp salt

20 g unsalted butter, melted

1 whole spring chicken, about 700–800 g

1 tsp ground paprika

5 g English parsley, finely chopped

VEGETABLES

1 carrot, diced

1 broccoli, stem removed, diced

100 g shiitake mushrooms, stems removed, diced

2 tsp minced garlic

20 g unsalted butter, melted

4 tsp salt

1 tsp ground black pepper

In a bowl, mix garlic, onion, dried shiitake mushroom bits, thyme, pepper, salt and butter together. Rub chicken inside and out with mixture, pouring any leftover into the cavity. Place on a tray, cover and refrigerate overnight or at least 30 minutes.

Preheat the oven to 180°C.

On a roasting tray, place carrot, broccoli and mushrooms. Add garlic, butter, salt and pepper, then toss to coat.

Place chicken on top of vegetables and cover tray with aluminium foil. Roast for 18–20 minutes.

Remove tray from oven and carefully transfer vegetables to a serving bowl. Return chicken to oven and roast uncovered for another 10 minutes at 180°C until golden brown.

Garnish with paprika and parsley. Serve warm with roasted vegetables.

Lemon and White Wine Baked Fish

Makes 2–3 portions

2–3 fish fillets, about 400–500 g
(sea bass or salmon works
well for this recipe, but feel free
to try other types of fish that
you prefer)

$^1/_2$ lemon, cut into 6 slices

200–300 g asparagus,
ends trimmed

120 ml white wine

150 ml cooking cream

6 cloves garlic, peeled
and minced

10 g English parsley, chopped

A pinch of ground paprika

Preheat the oven to 180°C. Line a baking tray with
aluminium foil.

Arrange fish fillets on prepared tray. Place lemon slices and
asparagus around fillets, then pour wine and cream over. Top
with minced garlic. Bake for 15 minutes.

You can also steam this in a rice cooker. Use aluminium
foil to make a parcel for the fish, lemon, asparagus and
seasoning. Prepare rice as you would normally. Add water to
rice cooker pot, then place steaming rack over rice. Place foil
parcel on rack and use the regular setting for cooking rice.

Transfer fish fillets to individual plates. Top with asparagus or
serve it on the side.

Pour creamy cooking liquid into a saucepan over low heat.
Simmer while adjusting seasoning to taste. Cover fish with
sauce, then garnish with some parsley and paprika.

As a chef and restaurant owner, I like to cook for others, but when it comes to my own meals, I get lazy! On one of my off-days, I was dragging my feet to go out for dinner, yet I didn't want to order in because that would typically mean soggy or lukewarm food. I went to the kitchen and found some white wine and frozen fish fillets, so I threw them and some seasoning on a baking tray and put it in the oven. It turned out surprisingly well! Since then, I've always joked that the name of this dish should really be "Lazy Baked Fish".

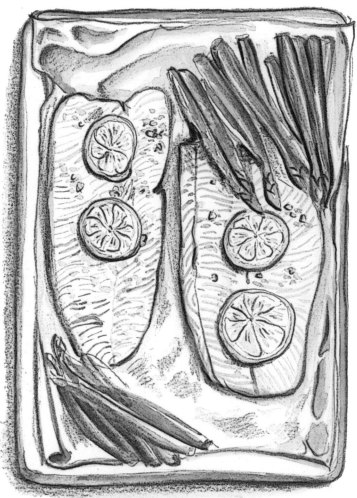

Whenever I have dinner with friends at a *zi char* stall, I see other diners ordering this dish. It's very popular because, of course, it's delicious! But it can be quite pricey, and sometimes the prawns served may not be the best. So why not make it at home, where you can ensure you'll be using the freshest ingredients. It's super easy to put together.

Home-style Cereal Prawns

Makes 2–3 portions served with rice

Vegetable oil as needed

2 Tbsp cornflour

2 Tbsp all-purpose (plain) flour

2 tsp salt

1 egg

16 tiger prawns, rinsed and pat dry

100 g instant cereal

1 Tbsp milk powder

1 Tbsp sugar

1 tsp ground white pepper

70 g unsalted butter

3 g curry leaves

2 bird's eye chillies (*cili padi*), diced, optional

Heat enough oil for deep-frying in a pot over medium heat.

Meanwhile, combine cornflour, all-purpose flour and 1 tsp salt in a medium bowl and mix well. In a separate bowl, beat egg well.

Dip a prawn in the egg before dredging it through the flour mixture to coat. Repeat to coat all the prawns.

When oil is hot, add prawns and deep-fry until golden yellow. Do this in batches so that you do not overcrowd the pot. Set aside deep-fried prawns on paper towels to drain excess oil.

In a bowl, combine cereal, milk powder, sugar, pepper and the remaining salt. Set aside.

In a large frying pan over medium heat, melt butter with 1 Tbsp oil. Add curry leaves and bird's eye chillies, stir-frying for 1 minute. Add cereal mixture and fry for 2 minutes until everything is well mixed.

Finally, add prawns and fry lightly until prawns are well coated with crispy cereal mixture.

Ketchup Prawns

Makes 2–3 portions served with rice

16 tiger prawns, rinsed and
    pat dry

1 tsp salt

1 tsp ground white pepper

Vegetable oil as needed

2 large yellow onions, peeled
    and diced

1 clove garlic, peeled and minced

2 slices peeled ginger

2 Tbsp Shaoxing wine

2 tsp sugar

$1/2$ bottle ketchup,
    about 150–170 g

1 Tbsp sweet chilli sauce

120 ml water

1 stalk spring onion, sliced

Rub prawns with salt and pepper, then leave to sit for
15 minutes.

Heat enough oil for deep-frying in a pot over medium heat.
When oil is hot, add prawns, a few at a time, and deep-
fry 1–2 minutes until crispy. The prawns will not be cooked
through. Transfer fried prawns onto a paper towel to absorb
excess oil.

In a frying pan over medium heat, add 1 Tbsp oil. Fry onion,
garlic and ginger until fragrant, then add prawns, Shaoxing
wine and sugar. Adjust heat to high and sauté for 1 minute.

Add ketchup, chilli sauce and water, stirring to combine and
coat prawns evenly. Simmer over high heat until sauce is
slightly thickened.

Transfer to a serving plate and garnish with spring onion.

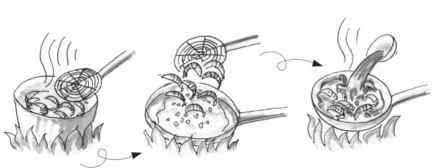

A dish with ketchup is often something that reminds many adults of their childhood (sweet and sour anything, or fries with lots of ketchup!). For me, this takes me back to the rare occasion my parents came home with tiger prawns for dinner — prawns were expensive and difficult for a low-income family to afford. My mum turned the prawns into this delicious dish with the help of a bottle of ketchup. But that wasn't the only high point of the night for my siblings and I: after dinner, a small truck arrived at our house to deliver a 42-inch colour TV. It turned out that my father had struck the lottery recently, and the prawns and TV were treats for the family. Now, whenever I have this dish, I think of that night we got our first colour TV.

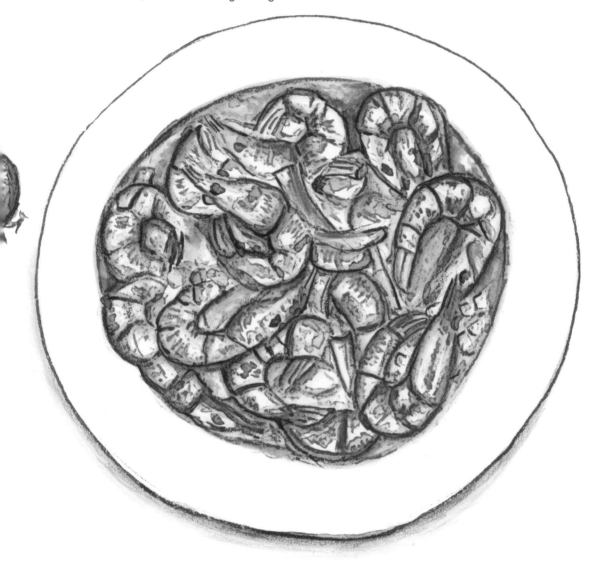

In Chinese cooking, noodles are often seasoned heavily with oyster sauce and dark soy sauce. The first pasta dish I had was vongole pasta, and it contributed to my realisation that noodles can be treated lightly so that the amazing flavours of the other ingredients can stand out. These noodles come together really quickly, which means it'll be a staple for busy home cooks.

Pasta Vongole with White Wine Sauce

Makes 2–3 portions

1 kg clams

Salt as needed

250 g pasta
(linguine / angel hair)

4 Tbsp olive oil

4 cloves garlic, peeled
and minced

1 sweet yellow onion, peeled
and diced

1 green bell pepper (capsicum),
diced

1 red bell pepper (capsicum),
diced

120 ml white wine

700 ml chicken stock or water

1 tsp ground white pepper

10 g English parsley,
finely chopped

In a large bowl or pot, submerge clams in salted water and set aside for 30 minutes. This process helps the shells to open up slightly and release sand.

Meanwhile, bring a pot of water to a boil and cook pasta according to the instructions on the packaging. Linguine usually takes 6–7 minutes, while angel hair should take about 5 minutes. Transfer cooked pasta into a bowl of iced water, then drain well. Place pasta in a bowl and toss with 2 Tbsp olive oil to prevent sticking. Set aside.

Drain clams.

Heat 2 Tbsp olive oil in a frying pan over medium heat. Fry garlic and onion until fragrant. Add bell peppers and stir-fry for 2 minutes before adding clams and adjusting heat to high.

Pour in white wine and cook mixture until fragrant and clams start opening up. Add stock and simmer for 2 minutes. Remove clams from mixture and set aside.

Adjust heat to medium-high, then season clam stock with pepper and 2 tsp salt. Add pasta to stock and cook for 1 minute.

Portion into individual dishes, top with clams, then pour clam stock over pasta. Serve warm.

Aglio Olio Laksa Pasta

Makes 2–3 portions

7 Tbsp + 100 ml olive oil

1 tsp salt

250 g linguine or angel hair pasta

3 eggs, at room temperature

100 g dried prawns

50 g + 20 g laksa leaves, stems removed

2 cloves garlic, peeled

50 g candle nuts

1 stalk lemongrass, chopped

8–10 prawns, shells removed and reserved, deveined

250 ml cooking cream

2 *tau pok* (deep-fried beancurd puff), cut into 8 slices

1 large deep-fried fish cake, about 80 g, sliced

1 Tbsp dried chilli flakes

Fill a pot with water. Add 1 Tbsp olive oil and a pinch of salt. Bring to a boil and add pasta, stirring briefly to ensure pasta does not stick to the bottom of the pot. Cook according to the instructions on the packaging. Transfer cooked pasta into a bowl of iced water, then drain well. Place pasta in a bowl and toss with 2 Tbsp olive oil to prevent sticking. Set aside.

Bring a small pot of water to a boil. When water is boiling, add eggs, cover and cook for 15 minutes. Leave to cool. Peel and slice into halves. Set aside.

Place dried prawns, 50 g laksa leaves, garlic, candle nuts, lemongrass and 100 ml olive oil in a food processor and blend until a paste forms. Set aside spice paste.

In a frying pan over medium heat, add 4 Tbsp olive oil. Fry reserved prawn shells until they turn orange and fragrant. Turn off the heat, discard shells and transfer half of the prawn oil into a dish.

Return the frying pan to medium heat and fry prawns in the remaining prawn oil. When prawns are half-cooked, add cooking cream followed by spice paste. Adjust heat to high and bring to a boil, stirring constantly. Add *tau pok*, return sauce to a boil, then remove from heat.

In another pot, bring water to a boil and poach pasta briefly. Drain and transfer to individual bowls. Ladle sauce over pasta and top with eggs and fish cake.

Chop 20 g laksa leaves. Sprinkle over pasta, along with chilli flakes, then drizzle the reserved prawn oil over.

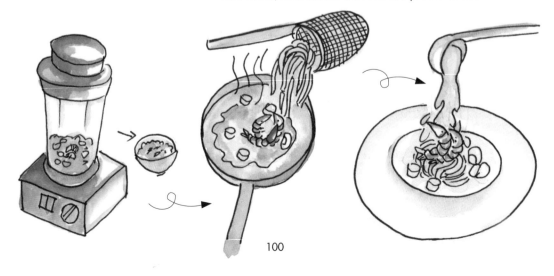

Most people would assume that a fusion dish like laksa pasta would take the form of Italian noodles in a thick soupy laksa sauce. Since the laksa spice paste is so fragrant on its own, I tried to make a version of laksa pasta that focused on it, replacing the coconut milk with cooking cream. The result is a creaminess that's robust but not overpowering, letting the fragrant laksa flavour shine.

I love that this dish is a visual feast as well as a hearty meal bursting with flavours. It is a saffron-infused seafood paella loaded with mussels, scallops and prawns. I also use a mix of white and brown rice, which gives the dish extra colour while making it a little healthier.

Seafood Paella

Makes 2–3 portions

3 Tbsp olive oil

8–10 tiger prawns, peeled and shells reserved

20 g garlic, peeled and diced

1 sweet yellow onion, peeled and diced

200 g bell pepper (capsicum), diced

1$^1/_2$ cups uncooked white rice

$^1/_2$ cup uncooked brown rice

10 mussels

100 g scallops

100 ml white wine

800 ml chicken stock

5 tomatoes, diced

5 g saffron

2 tsp ground paprika

Spring onion for garnishing, chopped

Coriander leaves for garnishing, chopped

Heat oil in a frying pan over medium heat. Fry reserved prawn shells until they turn orange and fragrant. Discard shells, keeping prawn oil in frying pan.

Add garlic, onion and bell pepper, then stir-fry until fragrant.

Add white rice, brown rice, prawns, mussels, scallops and white wine, then stir-fry until mixture is fragrant, about 10 minutes.

Transfer to a rice cooker, then add stock, tomatoes, saffron and paprika. Use the regular setting for cooking rice.

When rice is ready, portion to serve and garnish with spring onion and coriander.

Samsui Chicken

Makes 2–3 portions

1 whole chicken, about
    900 g–1 kg, washed
    and cleaned

3 cloves garlic, peeled and
    smashed

4 slices peeled ginger

2 Tbsp Shaoxing wine

1 tsp sesame oil

1 Tbsp salt

1 cucumber, sliced

1 head iceberg lettuce, leaves
    separated

GINGER SAUCE

400 ml olive oil

50 g garlic, peeled and minced

50 g ginger, peeled and minced

4 tsp salt

2 tsp sugar

1 Tbsp oyster sauce

100 g spring onion, chopped

100 g coriander, stems removed,
    chopped

Fill a large pot halfway with water (enough to submerge chicken later) and bring to a boil. Add garlic, ginger, Shaoxing wine, sesame oil and salt.

Holding the chicken by its neck, lower it into the boiling water briefly, then lift it up. Do this twice more before submerging chicken entirely in the water. Adjust heat to low, cover pot and leave to simmer for 30–40 minutes.

Pierce chicken thigh with a chopstick to check if it's cooked through. The chopstick should pierce the meat easily and there should be no blood. Remove chicken and place in a bowl of iced water immediately to stop the cooking.

Prepare ginger sauce. Heat oil in a frying pan over low heat. Fry garlic and ginger until fragrant, then add salt, sugar and oyster sauce, followed by spring onion and coriander. Stir to combine and remove from heat.

To carve the chicken, chop off its neck, wings and thighs. Carefully detach the breast meat from the bones in 2 halves. Make a small cut at the end of each thigh and detach the meat from the bones. Chop breast and thigh meat into bite-sized pieces. Arrange on a serving plate, garnish with cucumber slices and serve with lettuce leaves.

To eat, place a piece of chicken on top of a lettuce leaf and spoon sauce over. Bon appétit!

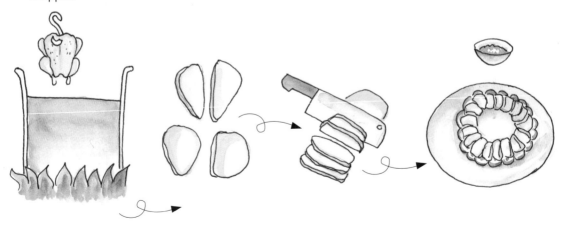

When I was a child, I looked forward to every Chinese New Year, particularly the night before it because my mum would cook a sumptuous meal for reunion dinner. This dish was always on our table for reunion dinner, as well as those of our neighbours, and I loved it the most. Back then, I didn't know its name and origin, but now that I do, it makes sense. Many families in my village were Hakka, and this dish was apparently made by Hakka Samsui women.

Cantonese Bak Chang

Makes about 30 dumplings

60 dried bamboo leaves, soaked overnight to soften

Reed string for tying, soaked overnight to soften (substitute with hemp string or cooking twine)

RICE
2 Tbsp olive oil

2 Tbsp dried prawns

20 g minced garlic

30 g onion, peeled and minced

1 kg glutinous rice, soaked overnight

2–3 tsp salt

2 Tbsp dark soy sauce

2 Tbsp light soy sauce

FILLING
1.5–1.7 kg pork shoulder, cleaned and cut into cubes

2 Tbsp dark soy sauce

4 Tbsp light soy sauce

2 tsp ground white pepper

2 tsp five-spice powder

2 Tbsp oyster sauce

2 Tbsp Shaoxing wine

1 tsp salt

1 Tbsp vegetable oil

300 g black-eyed peas, soaked overnight in water with a pinch of salt, drained

300 g dried shiitake mushrooms, soaked for 20 minutes, drained and cut into cubes

30 salted egg yolks

FRIED CONDIMENTS
Vegetable oil as needed

100 g garlic, peeled and sliced

400 g shallot, peeled and sliced

400 g dried prawns, rinsed, drained and dried

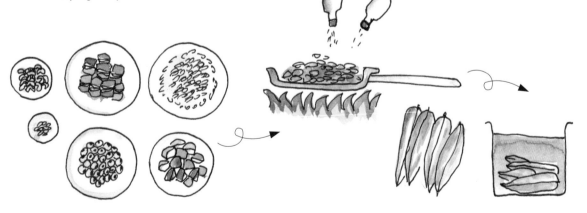

Prepare rice. Heat oil in a frying pan over medium heat. Fry dried prawns, garlic and onion until fragrant. Adjust heat to low, add rice and fry for 5–7 minutes. Season with salt and both soy sauces. Set aside.

Prepare filling. Place pork cubes in a large bowl and add both soy sauces, 1 tsp pepper, 1 tsp five-spice powder, oyster sauce and Shaoxing wine. Leave to marinate for at least 30 minutes.

Heat oil in a frying pan over medium heat and fry marinated pork cubes until meat changes colour. The meat will not be cooked through. Set aside.

In the same frying pan, fry black-eyed peas with salt, and the remaining five-spice powder and pepper until fragrant. Set aside.

Prepare fried condiments. Heat enough oil for covering garlic and shallots in a frying pan over low heat. Add garlic and shallots, then pan-fry until golden brown. Set aside.

In the same pan, pan-fry dried prawns until golden brown. Set aside.

To wrap a dumpling, place a bamboo leaf on top of another, then fold both short edges of the leaves together, overlapping them to form a cone. It should be large enough to fit in your palm.

Scoop a spoonful of rice into the cone and pack it gently into the bottom. Add a spoonful each of pork, black-eyed peas and mushrooms, followed by fried condiments and a salted egg yolk. Top with another spoonful of rice.

Wrap bamboo leaves around the rice to seal dumpling and form a pyramid. Secure leaves in place with reed string, but do not tie it too tightly, as the rice will expand as it cooks.

Bring a large pot of water to a boil. When water is boiling, submerge dumplings and adjust to medium heat. Cover and boil dumplings for 3 hours, checking the water level occasionally. Top up pot with more hot water to make sure dumplings are fully covered.

Remove from heat and hang dumplings to dry until bamboo leaves are dry to the touch. These are best eaten warm.

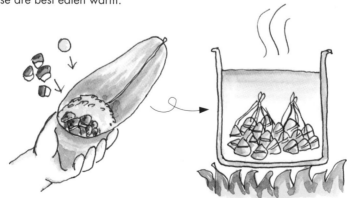

There are a few types of savoury *chang* (rice dumplings), all of which differ in their fillings. The ones that my mum makes are, of course, Cantonese *bak chang*. Compared to *kee chang* (page 45), these are more troublesome to make because of the slightly complicated filling. But they are worth the effort! I would prepare the filling and rice in the morning and spend the afternoon wrapping the *chang*. It can be quite therapeutic if you've got everything ready for assembling. Make a big batch because these can be frozen and reheated by steaming. Or you can stick with tradition and give them away to family and friends.

ABOUT THE AUTHOR

Bill Ho's life as a chef began by accident. He studied graphic design at Saito University College in Petaling Jaya, Malaysia, but was waiting tables at a Chinese restaurant in Kuala Lumpur, working his way up from waiter to manager. One day, when the kitchen was short on staff, he picked up an apron to lend a hand, and discovered that cooking delicious food for customers was something he enjoyed. Since then, he has trained and worked as a chef in bars and restaurants, including the Royal Copenhagen Tea Lounge in Singapore.

Armed with several years of experience in the food industry, and a passion for creating fusion fare, Bill opened Eight Café and Bar in 2008. He continues to develop dishes for its menu and lends a personal touch to the café's décor with his sketches and paintings. Connect with Bill on Instagram @Bill8Cafe, where he shares about food and art at his café.

WEIGHTS AND MEASURES

Quantities for this book are given in Metric, Imperial and American (spoon) measures. Standard spoon and cup measurements used are: 1 tsp = 5 ml, 1 Tbsp = 15 ml, 1 cup = 250 ml. All measures are level unless otherwise stated.

LIQUID AND VOLUME MEASURES

Metric	Imperial	American
5 ml	$1/6$ fl oz	1 teaspoon
10 ml	$1/3$ fl oz	1 dessertspoon
15 ml	$1/2$ fl oz	1 tablespoon
60 ml	2 fl oz	$1/4$ cup (4 tablespoons)
85 ml	$2^1/2$ fl oz	$1/3$ cup
90 ml	3 fl oz	$3/8$ cup (6 tablespoons)
125 ml	4 fl oz	$1/2$ cup
180 ml	6 fl oz	$3/4$ cup
250 ml	8 fl oz	1 cup
300 ml	10 fl oz ($1/2$ pint)	$1^1/4$ cups
375 ml	12 fl oz	$1^1/2$ cups
435 ml	14 fl oz	$1^3/4$ cups
500 ml	16 fl oz	2 cups
625 ml	20 fl oz (1 pint)	$2^1/2$ cups
750 ml	24 fl oz ($1^1/5$ pints)	3 cups
1 litre	32 fl oz ($1^3/5$ pints)	4 cups
1.25 litres	40 fl oz (2 pints)	5 cups
1.5 litres	48 fl oz ($2^2/5$ pints)	6 cups
2.5 litres	80 fl oz (4 pints)	10 cups

DRY MEASURES

Metric	Imperial
30 grams	1 ounce
45 grams	$1^1/2$ ounces
55 grams	2 ounces
70 grams	$2^1/2$ ounces
85 grams	3 ounces
100 grams	$3^1/2$ ounces
110 grams	4 ounces
125 grams	$4^1/2$ ounces
140 grams	5 ounces
280 grams	10 ounces
450 grams	16 ounces (1 pound)
500 grams	1 pound, $1^1/2$ ounces
700 grams	$1^1/2$ pounds
800 grams	$1^3/4$ pounds
1 kilogram	2 pounds, 3 ounces
1.5 kilograms	3 pounds, $4^1/2$ ounces
2 kilograms	4 pounds, 6 ounces

OVEN TEMPERATURE

	°C	°F	Gas Regulo
Very slow	120	250	1
Slow	150	300	2
Moderately slow	160	325	3
Moderate	180	350	4
Moderately hot	190/200	370/400	5/6
Hot	210/220	410/440	6/7
Very hot	230	450	8
Super hot	250/290	475/550	9/10

LENGTH

Metric	Imperial
0.5 cm	$1/4$ inch
1 cm	$1/2$ inch
1.5 cm	$3/4$ inch
2.5 cm	1 inch